CONTENTS

PRODUCED BY THE WARHAMMER STUDIO
With thanks to the Faithful and the Warhammer Age of Sigmar community for their playtesting services.

Games Workshop Ltd., Willow Road, Lenton, Nottingham, NG7 2WS, United Kingdom
games-workshop.com

TO WAR!

Welcome to the *General's Handbook 2020*, a guide to playing games in the Mortal Realms. Packed with inspiration and brimming with battles, this volume explores all kinds of new and interesting ways for you to enjoy Warhammer Age of Sigmar.

This book expands on the Warhammer Age of Sigmar core rules to support an array of gaming styles that suit all hobbyists, from casual collectors who play occasional games with their friends to veteran warriors who spend years honing their forces for competitive tournaments.

Everyone enjoys the Games Workshop hobby in different ways. Some are avid painters who collect stunning centrepiece models, while others immerse themselves in gripping tales of the realms. For some, though, using their collections to play games against like-minded opponents across the tabletop is at the very heart of their hobby. If you fall into the latter category, then this book is for you, as it focuses on that aspect of the hobby where the miniatures meet the battlefield.

It is important to note that all of the rules presented in this book are optional; they can be used, or not, in any combination that you and your tabletop adversaries find enjoyable. To this end, the *General's Handbook 2020* has been designed to work as a gaming toolbox, providing many options to get the dice rolling and play with your collection of Citadel Miniatures on the tabletop.

The different ways to combine the rules in this book are practically endless, and this flexible system ensures that everyone can find a style of play that suits them. The *General's Handbook 2020* has been designed with a particular focus on team gaming and doubles events in mind; if you're looking to run exciting multiplayer battles, you'll find a swathe of content in this book alongside plenty of new rules for traditional one-on-one gaming.

Whether you've just picked up your first Start Collecting! box or are dusting off a collection from days long past, the *General's Handbook 2020* is here to help you find your favourite way of playing.

THREE WAYS TO PLAY

The first three sections of this book provide rules for three different gaming styles: open play, narrative play and matched play.

OPEN PLAY

Open play is the first type of play that is covered, and it is the most flexible style because it can be as simple or as complex as you like. Simply pick any Citadel Miniatures and start playing.

In the open play section (pg 6-43), you'll find all the rules for playing Skies of Slaughter – a fantastic new way of using your Age of Sigmar miniatures to fight deadly high-octane dogfights in the skies of the Mortal Realms. There are even rules for running Skies of Slaughter campaigns that feature whole wings of fighters, where your favourite flying monsters will grow in power the more games you play with them.

NARRATIVE PLAY

Narrative play is based around the stories of the Mortal Realms, either those you can read in our books or those you write yourself. Narrative play can involve one-off battles fought between mighty heroes or multiple games linked via a campaign. In the narrative play section (pg 44-67), you will find a suite of special rules that you

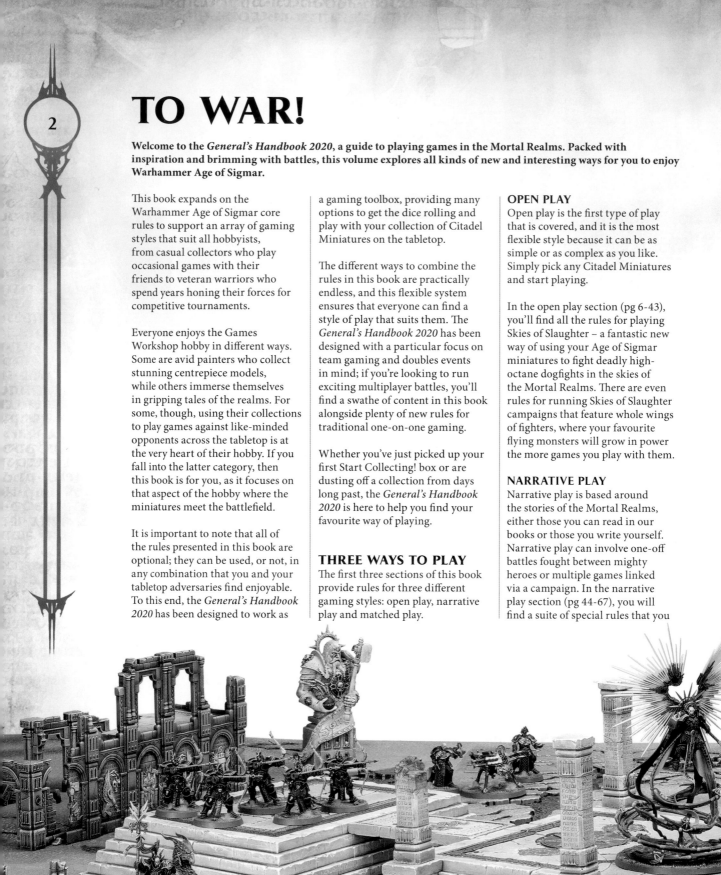

can 'plug in' to lend an immediate narrative to any team battle. For those looking to take doubles gaming further, the Whisper Engine campaign focuses on and celebrates team gaming, challenging you and your friends to use all your cunning and scheme your way to victory!

This section also contains the Anvil of Apotheosis, a toolbox with which you can create your own legendary characters to battle in the Mortal Realms. This system has been designed to be quick, easy and fun to use – the combinations of mounts, weapons and abilities are vast, so if you can dream of a cool character to lead your army to glorious victory, you'll have all the resources you need to bring them to life on the tabletop.

MATCHED PLAY

Matched play allows armies to be tested against each other under conditions that give no particular advantage to either side, so you can see which army is strongest and which general is canniest. These styles are fluid and their component parts can often be used together, depending on what you are trying to achieve.

In the matched play section (pg 68-109), you will find updated Pitched Battle and Meeting Engagement rules, including revised and rebalanced battleplans, as well as

THE MOST IMPORTANT RULE

In a game as detailed and wide-ranging as Warhammer Age of Sigmar, there may be times when you are not sure exactly how to resolve a situation that has come up during play.

When this happens, have a quick chat with your opponent and apply the solution that makes the most sense to you both (or seems the most fun!).

If no single solution presents itself, both of you should roll a dice, and whoever rolls higher gets to choose what happens. This means you can swiftly and easily resolve the issue, allowing you both to get on with the fighting!

matched play rules for team gaming. Also included is a suite of rules for fighting in different Mortal Realms. In the accompanying booklet, *Pitched Battle Profiles 2020*, you will find updated Pitched Battle points for all available units.

The final section of this book is called Conquest Unbound (pg 110-129) and offers a variety of tournament packs for different styles of matched play events, allowing you to lead your army to victory in competitive play. Also included is an Open War army generator, enabling you to quickly create a force and get straight into the action.

Whatever style of game you choose and however you use your miniatures, there is no right or wrong way to play Warhammer Age of Sigmar, so long as everyone adheres to the Most Important Rule. We're all here to have fun, after all!

THE PLAYER'S CODE

There is a famous adage that goes 'it matters not if you win or lose, it's how you play the game.' It is in this spirit that Warhammer Age of Sigmar is intended to be played.

We believe that Warhammer Age of Sigmar is a game best played in the right spirit, but sometimes it can be difficult to know what playing in the right spirit actually means. To help with this, we've put together a set of guidelines that we call 'The Warhammer Age of Sigmar Player's Code', opposite.

So, what inspired the Player's Code? Well, it all began as we wrestled with the rules for running Warhammer Age of Sigmar tournaments. One of the things we were keen for the rules to prevent was deliberate time-wasting, where a player takes ages over their turn in order to get some kind of advantage. Most players know that time-wasting is completely against the spirit of the game, but sometimes this principle gets ignored in the white heat of a competitive tournament.

However, we struggled to write robust rules that stopped time-wasting from occurring. What we needed was a different way of dealing with the practice. By a lucky coincidence, one of the members of the rules team had recently watched a documentary about a psychological test, which looked at how many people would choose to cheat in order to win a small amount of money.

The test was carried out at two American universities, both of which had codes of conduct that all students had signed up to and that included a proviso about being honest and truthful. What the

researchers found was that under normal circumstances, most people were prepared to cheat at the test, but if they reminded people of the honour code they had signed, it reduced the amount of cheating to zero.

The lesson was clear: most people want to do the right thing, but occasionally they need to be reminded of what that is in order to avoid temptation.

So we decided to simply put together a code of conduct for players of Warhammer Age of Sigmar and to ask players to read it and follow it when playing their games. In many tournaments, you will be given a copy of the code before you start playing, just to help you keep these principles in mind.

If you look at the Player's Code, you'll see that it is split into cardinal rules and principles. In order to uphold the code, the cardinal rules are all you really need to follow, as the principles are really just examples of the cardinal rules in practice. And to be honest, there is one guideline in the code that is

more important than the others, which is treating your opponent with respect – after all, being impolite, telling untruths and cheating are hardly respectful.

Everything else in the code is important too, of course, mainly because it is sometimes hard to draw the line between things that are okay to do during a game and things that you should avoid doing, and they will help you to draw that line. However, if you want to play the game in the right spirit, then being respectful of your opponent should be more important to you than winning.

By now, some of you may be thinking, 'Well that's all well and good, but does this mean I'm not allowed to try and win the games I play?' This is a very fair question, so just to make things clear, the code does not mean you shouldn't try to win your games – you absolutely should – but rather that there is a right and a wrong way to go about it.

That's why we have not presented the Player's Code as a set of rules that you must follow, like the core rules. The Player's Code is more personal, and the skills it promotes are something you can work away at and improve on over time. If you do so, you'll find yourself having more enjoyable games, and what's more, you'll be playing the game as it's *meant* to be played – an enjoyable and stimulating pastime where games are played in a spirit of friendly rivalry.

THE WARHAMMER AGE OF SIGMAR PLAYER'S CODE

CARDINAL RULES

- Always be polite and respectful.

- Always tell the truth and never cheat.

PRINCIPLES

- Arrive on time with all of the things you need to play the game.

- Make a respectful gesture to your opponent before and after the game, such as offering a handshake, fist bump, etc.

- Avoid using language your opponent might find offensive.

- Ask your opponent's permission if you wish to use unpainted models or proxy models.

- Offer your opponent a chance to examine your army roster before the battle starts.

- Answer any questions your opponent has about your army and the rules that apply to your army.

- Measure moves and distances carefully and accurately.

- Give your opponent the chance to examine your dice rolls before picking up the dice.

- Ask permission before touching any of your opponent's miniatures.

- Remind your opponent about rules they may have forgotten to use or that they have used incorrectly, especially when doing so is to your opponent's advantage rather than your own.

- Never deliberately waste time during a game.

- Avoid distracting an opponent when they are trying to concentrate, and be careful to respect their personal space.

- Never complain about your bad luck or your opponent's good luck.

- Never collude with an opponent to fix the outcome of a game.

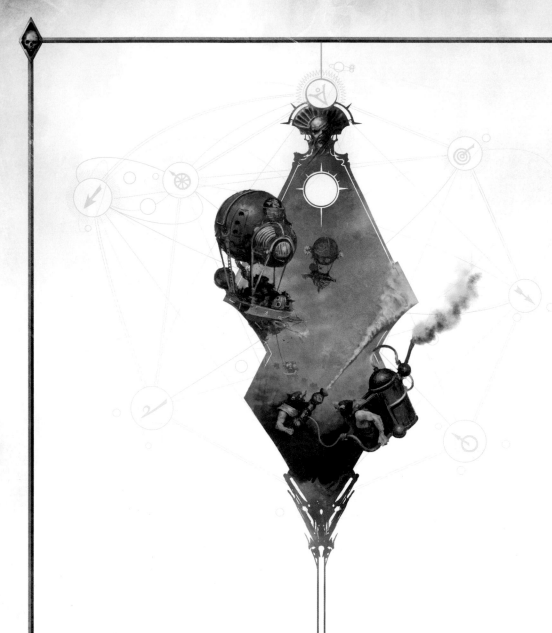

OPEN PLAY GAMES

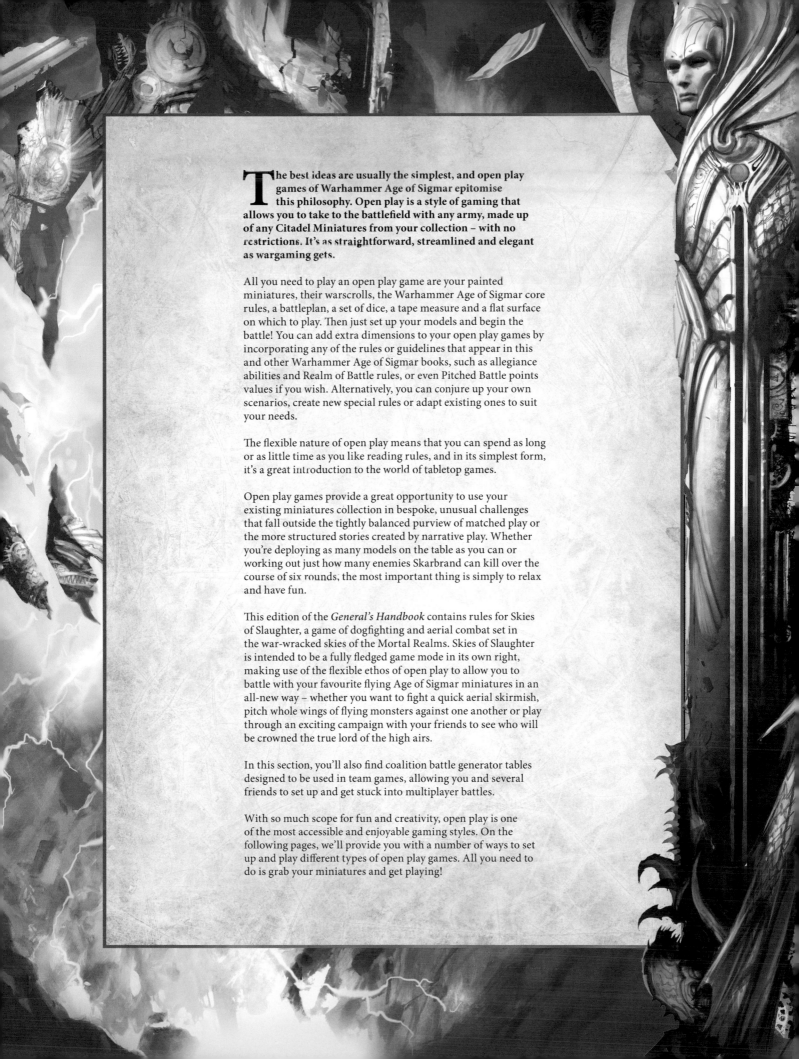

The best ideas are usually the simplest, and open play games of Warhammer Age of Sigmar epitomise this philosophy. Open play is a style of gaming that allows you to take to the battlefield with any army, made up of any Citadel Miniatures from your collection – with no restrictions. It's as straightforward, streamlined and elegant as wargaming gets.

All you need to play an open play game are your painted miniatures, their warscrolls, the Warhammer Age of Sigmar core rules, a battleplan, a set of dice, a tape measure and a flat surface on which to play. Then just set up your models and begin the battle! You can add extra dimensions to your open play games by incorporating any of the rules or guidelines that appear in this and other Warhammer Age of Sigmar books, such as allegiance abilities and Realm of Battle rules, or even Pitched Battle points values if you wish. Alternatively, you can conjure up your own scenarios, create new special rules or adapt existing ones to suit your needs.

The flexible nature of open play means that you can spend as long or as little time as you like reading rules, and in its simplest form, it's a great introduction to the world of tabletop games.

Open play games provide a great opportunity to use your existing miniatures collection in bespoke, unusual challenges that fall outside the tightly balanced purview of matched play or the more structured stories created by narrative play. Whether you're deploying as many models on the table as you can or working out just how many enemies Skarbrand can kill over the course of six rounds, the most important thing is simply to relax and have fun.

This edition of the *General's Handbook* contains rules for Skies of Slaughter, a game of dogfighting and aerial combat set in the war-wracked skies of the Mortal Realms. Skies of Slaughter is intended to be a fully fledged game mode in its own right, making use of the flexible ethos of open play to allow you to battle with your favourite flying Age of Sigmar miniatures in an all-new way – whether you want to fight a quick aerial skirmish, pitch whole wings of flying monsters against one another or play through an exciting campaign with your friends to see who will be crowned the true lord of the high airs.

In this section, you'll also find coalition battle generator tables designed to be used in team games, allowing you and several friends to set up and get stuck into multiplayer battles.

With so much scope for fun and creativity, open play is one of the most accessible and enjoyable gaming styles. On the following pages, we'll provide you with a number of ways to set up and play different types of open play games. All you need to do is grab your miniatures and get playing!

SKIES OF SLAUGHTER

Skies of Slaughter is a game of aerial combat in the Age of Sigmar, in which winged leviathans and gun-laden flying machines engage in thrilling airborne duels amidst the clouds high above the Mortal Realms.

THE MODELS

Skies of Slaughter is played using large flying models from the Warhammer Age of Sigmar range, referred to as **flying monsters** in the rules that follow.

PREPARING FOR PLAY

Skies of Slaughter can be played either by two players or by a large group of players taking part in one massive aerial battle!

Each player will need at least one flying monster and its warscroll. The player controls the actions of that flying monster during the battle and is referred to as the controlling player in the rules that follow. Players can choose to field a wing of two or more flying monsters if they wish.

Each player will also need a tape measure or ruler to measure weapon ranges and plenty of dice – enough to carry out the attacks that the flying monster makes during the battle as well as to record its velocity and any wounds it has suffered.

Games of Skies of Slaughter need a flat playing surface to represent the area where the battle takes place. A dining table makes an excellent battlefield for 2 to 6 flying monsters.

Larger games will need a bigger table or can be played on the floor (just be extra careful not to kick over any of your models in the heat of battle!).

Finally, you will need to pick a skybattle to play. We've included a selection in this book to get you started, but keep your eyes peeled for more in issues of White Dwarf. Duels are battles with one flying monster on each side, while Encounters are battles between more than two flying monsters. Once you've picked a skybattle and followed its set-up instructions, you are ready to start playing.

SKIES OF SLAUGHTER WARSCROLLS

Each type of flying monster in Skies of Slaughter has a warscroll, which lists everything you need to know about the flying monster during the game. You can find warscrolls for a wide selection of flying monsters at the end of these rules (pg 24-39).

1   **Name:** The name of the flying monster that the warscroll describes.

2   **Description:** An overview of the flying monster and how it fights.

3   **Flying Characteristics:** This set of characteristics tells you how fast the flying monster is, how many wounds it can sustain and how well it can prevent and recover from injuries.

4   **Weapons:** The weapons that the flying monster is armed with, followed by any weapon options it can use in italics.

5   **Weapon Characteristics:** These characteristics provide information about the flying monster's weapons.

6   **Special Rules:** These describe any additional rules or abilities that the flying monster has.

MANOEUVRE TABLE

Manoeuvre	Velocity			Execution
	2	3	4	
Level Flight	Always Safe			Move Move
Swerve	2+	3+	4+	Move Sideslip Move
Bank	2+	3+	4+	Move Move Turn
Turn	3+	4+	5+	Move Turn Move
Snap Turn	4+	5+	6+	Turn Move Move

7   **Manoeuvre Table:** This table shows all of the aerial manoeuvres the flying monster can perform, how dangerous they are to perform at different velocities, and how they are executed.

8   **Manoeuvre:** The name of each of the manoeuvres the flying monster can perform.

9   **Danger Rolls:** Sometimes a flying monster will have to make a danger roll before performing a manoeuvre. This is done by cross-referencing the velocity of the flying monster with the manoeuvre being performed.

10   **Execution:** This lists the Moves, Turns, Reversals and Sideslips the flying monster must carry out when it performs the manoeuvre.

SKIES OF SLAUGHTER SKYBATTLES

Skybattles include a set of instructions that describe how the battle is fought.

1   **Name and Overview:** The name and a brief description of the skybattle.

2   **Combatants:** The flying monsters that can be used in the skybattle.

3   **Set-up:** How the flying monsters are set up at the start of the skybattle.

4   **Special Rules:** Any special rules that apply to the skybattle.

5   **Victory Conditions:** How the winner of the skybattle is determined.

6   **Map:** The map illustrates how to set up the flying monsters at the start of the skybattle and anything else that may affect the skybattle's combat zone.

VELOCITIES

At the start of the battle, flying monsters are given a velocity of 1 to 6, determined by the skybattle being played. This is indicated by placing a dice at the front of the flying monster's base, as shown on the diagram, and may change as the battle progresses.

A flying monster's velocity can never be less than 1 or more than the maximum velocity on its warscroll. Changes to the flying monster's velocity that would cause this to happen are ignored.

SPINS

Should a flying monster's velocity ever fall to 1, it will go into a spin (pg 14). This can be an effective way to get away from the enemy, but if the flying monster doesn't pull out of the spin in time, it may crash into the ground!

FACING AND ARCS

A flying monster's **facing** – i.e. the direction it is pointing in – is important for determining how it turns and which weapons it can attack with. Turns (pg 12) and weapon arcs (pg 14) are split into 45-degree segments measured from the centre of the model's base, as shown in the diagrams.

SEQUENCE OF PLAY

After set-up is complete, the battle can start. The battle is fought in turns, each of which is split into 3 'mini-turns' called **impulses**. The impulses are carried out one after the other and followed by a recovery step.

Sequence of Play
- First Impulse
- Second Impulse
- Third Impulse
- Recovery

IMPULSES

In each impulse, flying monsters carry out 1 **action**. They do so in an order determined by their velocities, from high to low. So, any flying monsters with a velocity of 6 will go first in each impulse, followed by those with a velocity of 5, and so on.

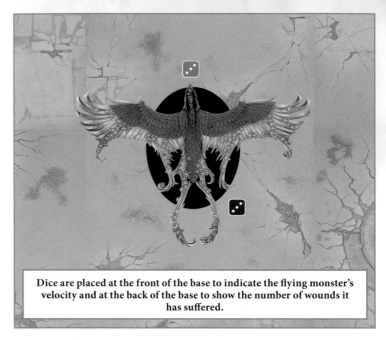

Dice are placed at the front of the base to indicate the flying monster's velocity and at the back of the base to show the number of wounds it has suffered.

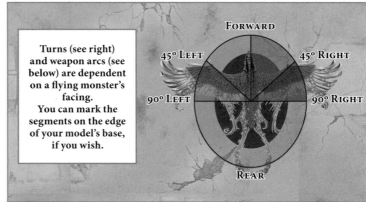

Turns (see right) and weapon arcs (see below) are dependent on a flying monster's facing.
You can mark the segments on the edge of your model's base, if you wish.

45° LEFT · 45° RIGHT · FORWARD · 90° LEFT · 90° RIGHT · REAR

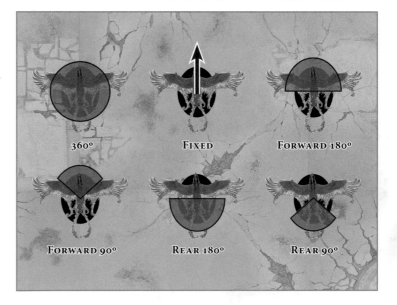

360° · FIXED · FORWARD 180° · FORWARD 90° · REAR 180° · REAR 90°

INITIATIVE ROLLS

Initiative rolls are made to determine the order in which flying monsters with the same velocity carry out actions. Each tied player rolls 2D6. The flying monster controlled by the player who rolled lowest carries out its action first (for flying monsters that are part of a wing, see page 17). Players tied for the lowest roll must roll again until there is only one player with the lowest roll. Any remaining tied players must repeat this process until all the flying monsters have carried out their actions.

ACTIONS

A flying monster's action is resolved in the following order:

1   The flying monster performs its manoeuvres.

2   The flying monster attacks.

3   Enemy flying monsters can retaliate.

4   The flying monster accelerates or brakes.

ONE ACTION PER IMPULSE

A flying monster cannot carry out more than 1 action per impulse. Once it has carried out its action, move the velocity dice to the back of the model's base to show that it has had its go. Return all of the flying monsters' velocity dice to the front at the start of the next impulse.

MANOEUVRES

Depending on its velocity, a flying monster may have to perform up to 2 **manoeuvres** as part of its action. Look up the flying monster's velocity on the Impulse Table to determine how many manoeuvres it *must* perform:

IMPULSE TABLE			
Velocity	First Impulse	Second Impulse	Third Impulse
6	Zoom!	Zoom!	Zoom!
5	Zoom!	Zoom!	Cruise
4	Zoom!	Cruise	Cruise
3	Cruise	Cruise	Cruise
2	Cruise	Cruise	Attack
1	Spin	Spin	Spin

Zoom!: Must perform 2 manoeuvres, then attack, then accelerate or brake.

Cruise: Must perform 1 manoeuvre, then attack, then accelerate or brake.

Attack: Attack, then accelerate or brake.

Spin: Spin (pg 14).

Note that a flying monster that is attacking or spinning cannot perform *any* manoeuvres.

DECLARING MANOEUVRES

You must declare the manoeuvre that a flying monster will perform before it executes it. If the flying monster must perform more than 1 manoeuvre, declare and perform the first one, then declare and perform the second one.

AVAILABLE MANOEUVRES

The manoeuvres a flying monster can perform are shown on its warscroll. Look up the flying monster's velocity on its Manoeuvre Table to see which manoeuvres it can perform. Manoeuvres marked 'N/A' cannot be performed at that velocity. All other manoeuvres can be attempted, though some may require you to make a danger roll.

DANGER ROLLS

Manoeuvres can cause wounds if the flying monster is moving too quickly. This is represented by a making a **danger roll** before performing each manoeuvre. To make a danger roll, roll a dice, then cross-reference the flying monster's velocity with the manoeuvre being performed on its Manoeuvre Table.

If the roll is equal to or greater than the number listed on the table, the manoeuvre has been performed safely. If the roll is less than the number listed on the table, the flying monster still performs the manoeuvre, but it suffers 1 wound (pg 14) and 1 is subtracted from its velocity (this may cause it to go into a spin in its next impulse).

Depending on a flying monster's velocity, it might be able to perform certain manoeuvres on a 1+. Such manoeuvres are always performed safely unless a negative modifier applies. Some other manoeuvres are noted as being 'Safe' or 'Always Safe' – you never have to make a danger roll for these manoeuvres.

PERFORMING A MANOEUVRE

Each manoeuvre requires a flying monster to carry out a certain number of Moves, Turns, Reversals and/or Sideslips. The number and order of the Moves, Turns, Reversals and Sideslips that must be carried out is listed in the Execution column for the manoeuvre on the flying monster's Manoeuvre Table. For example, a manoeuvre might require a flying monster to make 2 Moves and then 1 Turn.

Moves

To make a Move, pick the flying monster up, move it straight ahead, and place it back down so that the velocity dice is at the back of its base. The velocity dice is then returned to the front of its base.

Turns

To make a Turn, slide the velocity dice round the flying monster's base by up to 45 degrees to the left or right. Then, pivot the flying monster so that the velocity dice is at the front of its base. The Turns made by a flying monster when performing a manoeuvre can be less than 45 degrees. However, any Turns that are not part of a manoeuvre (for example, if the flying monster is forced to make a Turn as a result of a roll on the Damage Table) must be for the full 45 degrees.

Reversals

To carry out a Reversal, slide the velocity dice round the flying monster's base by 180 degrees. Then, pivot the flying monster so that the velocity dice is at the front of its base.

Sideslips

Sideslips allow a flying monster to move in a direction other than straight ahead. To carry out a Sideslip, slide the velocity dice round the flying monster's base to any position within the flying monster's Forward 180° weapon arc (pg 10). Then, pick the flying monster up and move it over the dice as shown in the diagram on the right. The velocity dice is then returned to the front of the flying monster's base. Note that the flying monster's facing does not change during a Sideslip.

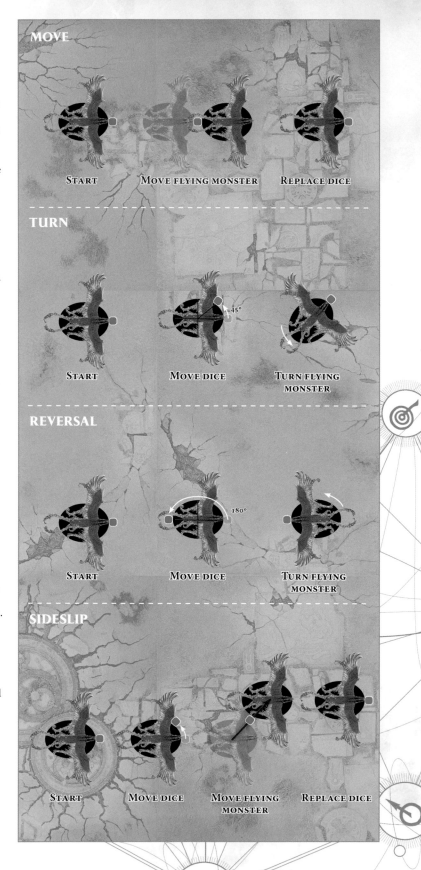

MOVE

START   MOVE FLYING MONSTER   REPLACE DICE

TURN

START   MOVE DICE   TURN FLYING MONSTER

REVERSAL

START   MOVE DICE   TURN FLYING MONSTER

SIDESLIP

START   MOVE DICE   MOVE FLYING MONSTER   REPLACE DICE

COLLISIONS

Flying monsters can manoeuvre over other flying monsters, but they cannot finish a manoeuvre touching any part of another flying monster (including its base). If this cannot be avoided, perform as much of the manoeuvre as possible, as shown in the diagram on the right, and then make a collision roll as described below. Carry out the same procedure if a 'forced' Move or Turn that occurs as a result of a spin or a roll on the Damage Table would result in two flying monsters touching.

To make a **collision roll**, the player controlling the manoeuvring flying monster rolls a dice. On a 1, the flying monsters have clipped each other, and they both suffer 1 wound (pg 14). If a flying monster collides with more than 1 other flying monster, make a collision roll for each.

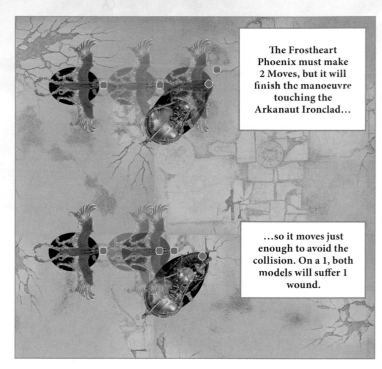

The Frostheart Phoenix must make 2 Moves, but it will finish the manoeuvre touching the Arkanaut Ironclad…

…so it moves just enough to avoid the collision. On a 1, both models will suffer 1 wound.

LEAVING THE BATTLE

Sometimes a flying monster may be forced to move off the edge of the battlefield. This is known as **leaving the battle**.

When this occurs, the controlling player removes the flying monster's model from the battlefield. They can then either decide that the monster will not return, or they can say that it will **loop back** and rejoin the fray.

If the flying monster loops back, leave its velocity dice on the battlefield to mark the point where it exited, and then roll 3 dice. For each 1, the flying monster suffers 1 wound. If it is not slain as a result of these dice rolls, the next time the flying monster would carry out an action, it can return.

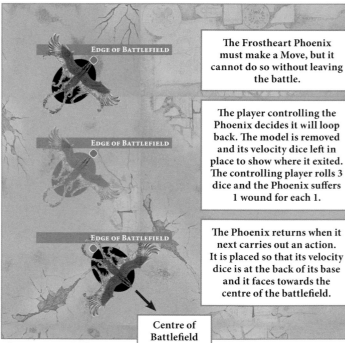

EDGE OF BATTLEFIELD

The Frostheart Phoenix must make a Move, but it cannot do so without leaving the battle.

EDGE OF BATTLEFIELD

The player controlling the Phoenix decides it will loop back. The model is removed and its velocity dice left in place to show where it exited. The controlling player rolls 3 dice and the Phoenix suffers 1 wound for each 1.

EDGE OF BATTLEFIELD

The Phoenix returns when it next carries out an action. It is placed so that its velocity dice is at the back of its base and it faces towards the centre of the battlefield.

Centre of Battlefield

When (or if!) the flying monster returns, place it back on the battlefield so that its velocity dice is at the back of its base and so that the flying monster is facing directly towards the centre of the battlefield, as shown in the diagram above. If this would result in a collision, slide the flying monster far enough to the left or right to avoid the other flying monster and then make a collision roll.

A flying monster cannot perform any manoeuvres nor attack in the impulse in which it returns; however, it can accelerate or brake.

SPINS

A flying monster goes into a **spin** if it has a velocity of 1 at the start of an action or if a roll on the Damage Table causes it to do so.

To carry out a spin, roll on the Spin Table. When a flying monster has to make **D3** Turns, roll a dice. On a 1-2, it makes 1 Turn; on a 3-4, it makes 2 Turns; and on a 5-6, it makes 3 Turns.

If the flying monster survives, make an acceleration roll for it (pg 16). On a 7+, the spin is brought under control; otherwise, the flying monster goes back into a spin. Keep on repeating this process – rolling on the Spin Table and making acceleration rolls – until the flying monster either brings the spin under control or is slain.

By bringing the spin under control, the flying monster increases its velocity by 1 (if it is possible for it to do so). If it was in a spin because it had a velocity of 1, bringing the spin under control counts as the flying monster's action. However, as it will now have a velocity of 2, it will not go into a spin in the next impulse.

SPIN TABLE	
D6	**Result**
1	**Crash to the Ground:** The flying monster is slain.
2-3	**Spin Left:** The flying monster makes D3 Turns to the left.
4-5	**Spin Right:** The flying monster makes D3 Turns to the right.
6	**Overdive:** The flying monster makes 1 Move and suffers 1 wound. If it is forced to leave the battle as a result, it is slain.

ATTACKS

After performing its manoeuvres, a flying monster can attack 1 enemy flying monster. The target must be within the range and weapon arc of at least 1 of the attacking model's weapons.

Range: Measure the range from the closest part of the attacking model to the closest part of the target model (including their bases).

Weapon Arc: A target can be attacked with a weapon if any part of the target model falls within that weapon's weapon arc (pg 10). If the weapon has a fixed weapon arc, in order to attack with that weapon, a straight line drawn through the centre of the attacking model in the direction it is facing must cross any part of the target model.

MAKING AN ATTACK

To make an attack, the controlling player rolls for each weapon that the target is within the range and weapon arc of. The number of dice that are rolled for a weapon are shown on the flying monster's warscroll (pg 24-39).

A hit is scored for each roll that is equal to or greater than the hit roll for the weapon listed on the flying monster's warscroll. Rolls of 1 always miss and rolls of 6 always hit.

If none of the attacking monster's weapons score any hits, the attack fails and has no effect on the target. Otherwise, damage is inflicted as described next.

INFLICTING DAMAGE

Add up the damage inflicted by the weapons that scored any hits and compare the total to the target's Toughness characteristic. Then, look up the result on the Attack Results Table.

THE DAMAGE TABLE

Sometimes the Attack Results Table will instruct the attacker to roll on the Damage Table. If it does so, roll 2D6 and look up the result on the Damage Table.

WOUNDS

Some results on the Attack Results Table cause the target to suffer wounds. Record the number of wounds suffered by placing a dice at the back of the flying monster's base. When the number of wounds suffered by a flying monster equals the Wounds characteristic on its warscroll, it is slain and removed from play.

ATTACK RESULTS TABLE	
Total damage is:	**Result**
Less than or equal to the target's Toughness	**Winged:** The attacker rolls once on the Damage Table.
Greater than the target's Toughness but not double	**Injured:** The target suffers 1 wound, and the attacker then rolls once on the Damage Table.
At least double the target's Toughness but not triple	**Seriously Injured:** The target suffers 2 wounds, and the attacker then rolls once on the Damage Table.
At least triple the target's Toughness	**Mortally Injured:** The target suffers 3 wounds, and the attacker then rolls once on the Damage Table.

DAMAGE TABLE

2D6	Result
2	**Multiple Hits:** The target suffers 1 wound. Then, roll on this table again.
3	**Tail Spin:** The target goes into a spin.
4	**Dodge:** Roll a dice. If the roll is less than the Wounds characteristic on the target's warscroll, the target suffers 1 wound.
5	**Zoom Forward:** Make an acceleration roll for the target. On a 7+, it makes 1 Move but does not change velocity. Otherwise, it suffers 1 wound.
6	**Swerve Left:** The target must make 1 Turn to the left.
7	**Press the Attack:** If the attacking monster is within 3" of the target, the attacker can choose to press the attack. If they do so, the attacker and the target each suffer 1 wound.
8	**Swerve Right:** The target must make 1 Turn to the right.
9	**Rear Up:** The target must either suffer 1 wound or lose 1 velocity (controlling player's choice).
10	**Falling Leaf:** The target must either suffer 1 wound or go into a spin (controlling player's choice).
11	**Critical Hit:** The target suffers 1 wound.
12	**Bullseye:** The target suffers D3 wounds.

ATTACK EXAMPLE

A Frostheart Phoenix attacks an Arkanaut Ironclad. The Phoenix is armed with Ice-cold Talons, which have a Forward 180° weapon arc and a range of 3". The distance between the Phoenix and the Ironclad is less than 3", and the Ironclad lies within the Phoenix's Forward 180° weapon arc, so it can attack with its Ice-cold Talons.

As shown on the Phoenix's warscroll, 5 dice must be rolled for its Ice-cold Talons, requiring rolls of 4 or more to hit. No modifiers apply, and 3 hits are scored. Each hit causes 2 damage, for a total of 6 damage inflicted on the Ironclad.

The Frostheart Phoenix attacks with its Ice-cold Talons, inflicting 6 damage on the Arkanaut Ironclad.

The damage inflicted by the attack exceeds but is not double the Ironclad's Toughness characteristic of 5. According to the Attack Results Table, this means that the Ironclad has been injured – it suffers 1 wound and the attacker must roll on the Damage Table.

The wound is recorded by placing a dice at the back of the Ironclad's base. The Ironclad has suffered 1 wound, so the dice is placed with the 1 facing up.

The attacker then rolls 2D6 on the Damage Table. The result is a 7 – Press the Attack. This means that if the attacking monster is within 3" of the target, then it can press the attack, causing the target to suffer 1 wound but also suffering 1 wound itself! The attacking player decides to press the attack, so the Ironclad suffers 1 additional wound and the Frostheart Phoenix suffers 1 wound.

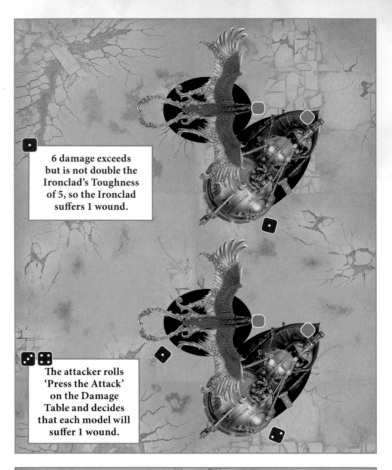

6 damage exceeds but is not double the Ironclad's Toughness of 5, so the Ironclad suffers 1 wound.

The attacker rolls 'Press the Attack' on the Damage Table and decides that each model will suffer 1 wound.

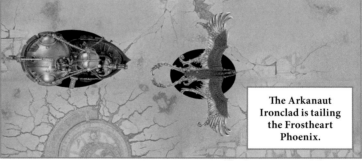

The Arkanaut Ironclad is tailing the Frostheart Phoenix.

TAILING
A flying monster is **tailing** its target if any part of its base is in the target's Rear 90° weapon arc and any part of the target's base is in the attacker's Forward 180° weapon arc. Add 1 to hit rolls for a flying monster that is tailing its target.

RETALIATION
After a flying monster has made its attack, the target can **retaliate** against the attacker, provided that it survived the attack and it has weapons that can be used against the target.

Retaliation attacks are carried out as described in the Attacks section, except that 1 is subtracted from all of the hit rolls, in addition to any other modifiers that apply.

ACCELERATING AND BRAKING
A flying monster is allowed to accelerate or brake after it has completed its manoeuvres and attacks (if any) and after any retaliation attacks have been made against it by the target.

Declare if you want your flying monster to accelerate or brake, and then make an **acceleration roll** or a **braking roll** by rolling 2D6. On a 7+, you can increase or decrease its velocity by 1 as appropriate. On a 3-6, its velocity is unchanged. On a 2 or less, its velocity is unchanged and the flying monster suffers 1 wound because of the stress and strain.

Remember that a flying monster's velocity can never be higher than the Velocity characteristic on its warscroll and that it will spin in its next impulse if it has a velocity of 1. If you accelerate when the flying monster's velocity is already at its maximum, the roll is wasted.

RECOVERY

Flying monsters are extremely tough and can recover from some of the injuries they have suffered if given enough time.

At the end of each impulse, after all actions have been completed, a **recovery roll** is made for each flying monster that has suffered any wounds. Roll 2D6 and compare it to the Recovery characteristic shown on the flying monster's warscroll. If the roll is equal to or greater than the Recovery characteristic, you can reduce the number of wounds that the flying monster has suffered by 1.

WINGS

A player can command more than 1 flying monster. The flying monsters that a player commands are collectively called a **wing**. Wings train and fight together and are able to provide each other with support.

If a player has a wing and several flying monsters from the wing have the same velocity at the start of an impulse, then the player makes 1 initiative roll (pg 11) for all of the flying monsters rather than rolling separately for each one. If the player's initiative roll is the lowest, they can pick any 1 of the flying monsters being rolled for to carry out its action first.

Just as importantly, if a flying monster from a player's wing is attacked, then any and all of the flying monsters from the wing that are able to attack are allowed to retaliate, not just the target flying monster.

SKYBATTLES

The flying monsters taking part in a game of Skies of Slaughter are taking part in a **skybattle**.

We've included 5 skybattles in this book. Two of the skybattles are called Duels – as their name implies, they pit 2 flying monsters against each other. Duels are ideal for quick one-on-one games and can easily be completed by experienced players in less than an hour.

There are also 2 skybattles called Encounters, which are designed for larger games with 3 or more flying monsters. Encounters can either be played by 2 players, with each player controlling a wing of 2 or more flying monsters, or between teams of players, where each player either controls a single flying monster or a wing.

For example, three players are new to Skies of Slaughter and each have a single flying monster, while the fourth player is a veteran with a wing of 3 flying monsters. They decide to fight an Encounter with the three players' flying monsters on one side and the fourth player's wing of 3 flying monsters on the other.

Finally, the skybattle 'Above the Gryphspine' is based on the background story included in this book. This skybattle is a little bit different to the Duels and Encounters, in that it requires the players to be able to field certain types of flying monster in order to recreate the story from the background (Duels and Encounters can be played with any flying monsters that are available).

That said, you can always use 'substitute' flying monsters to fill in for models you don't have in your collection or to allow more players to join the skybattle.

CHOOSING A SKYBATTLE

The players taking part in a game of Skies of Slaughter can choose to use any of the skybattles included in this book or in issues of White Dwarf – just decide among yourselves which skybattle you most want to play. Alternatively, you can let the dice decide by rolling on one of the following tables to determine which Duel or Encounter to play.

DUEL TABLE (2 FLYING MONSTERS)	
D6	Result
1-3	Chance Encounter
4-6	Death in the Skies

ENCOUNTER TABLE (3 OR MORE FLYING MONSTERS)	
D6	Result
1-3	Air War
4-6	Dawn Patrol

SKYBATTLE SPECIAL RULES

The following special rules cover unique situations not directly addressed by the Skies of Slaughter rules on the previous pages. They are only used if you have chosen a battleplan that specifically states that they are needed or in games of your own devising where you feel that it would be appropriate to include them.

GROUND ATTACK

Sometimes a skybattle will include ground targets that can be attacked by flying monsters. This will be stated in the skybattle instructions, along with the information needed to set up the ground targets at the start of the skybattle.

All ground targets have a **robustness value** and a **damage tolerance**, which tell you how tough they are and how much damage they can take. The robustness values and damage tolerances for the ground targets included in a skybattle will be stated in the skybattle instructions.

A flying monster can attack a ground target if the target is within its Forward 90° weapon arc at a range of up to 5". Attacking a ground target is very straightforward: roll 2D6 and add the Strafe values for each of the flying monster's weapons to the roll. Many weapons have a Strafe value of 0, but some will have a value of +1 or more. If a flying monster has several weapons with a value greater than 0, add all of them to the roll. For example, a Battlemage on Griffon

has two weapons with a Strafe value of 0, one with a value of +1 and one with a value of +2, so the controlling player would roll 2D6 and add 3 to the roll.

If the total roll, after any modifiers have been added, is equal to or greater than the ground target's robustness value, its damage tolerance is reduced by 1. Once its damage tolerance is reduced to 0, it is destroyed. Record the damage suffered by a ground target on a dice.

GROUND FIRE

Sometimes a ground target will have weapons it can use against enemy flying monsters. Each of these weapons will have a set of weapon characteristics like those found on the flying monsters' warscrolls.

Ground targets attack at the end of each impulse, after all the flying monsters have carried out their actions. Ground targets always attack the closest enemy flying monster that is within the range and weapon arc of at least 1 of their weapons. The

attack is made as normal (pg 14) – unless otherwise specified, the player whose flying monster is not under attack is the controlling player (if there is more than 1 such player, roll off to decide). Ground targets cannot 'Press the Attack' and must re-roll this result on the Damage Table. Flying monsters are not allowed to retaliate if they are attacked by ground fire.

LOW-LEVEL SKYBATTLES

Sometimes a skybattle will take place very close to the ground – these are known as 'low-level skybattles'. The terrain over which such a skybattle is taking place can be represented by scenery from your collection.

A flying monster cannot finish a manoeuvre touching a piece of scenery and must avoid it as if it were another flying monster. In the event of a collision (pg 13), make a collision roll just as you would with another flying monster, except that scenery hit by a flying monster does not suffer any damage.

FLOATING TERRAIN

Sometimes a skybattle will include areas of floating terrain; the skybattle instructions will say how the floating terrain must be set up. Floating terrain blocks both attacks and movement.

Attacks cannot be made if a line drawn from the centre of the attacker's base to the centre of the target's base passes across any floating terrain.

A flying monster cannot finish a manoeuvre touching an area of floating terrain and must avoid it as if it were another flying monster. In the event of a collision (pg 13), make a collision roll just as you would with another flying monster, except that floating terrain hit by a flying monster does not suffer any damage.

SKYBATTLE

DUEL: CHANCE ENCOUNTER

Two rivals are patrolling the skies, searching for their next kill. As fate would have it, they soon chance upon one another…

COMBATANTS

This skybattle is fought between 2 flying monsters.

SET-UP

Place the flying monsters in opposite corners of the battlefield, facing each other.

Both flying monsters start the battle with a velocity of 3.

VICTORY CONDITIONS

The flying monster that slays their opponent wins the battle. The battle is a draw if either flying monster leaves the battle and does not return.

SKYBATTLE

DUEL: DEATH IN THE SKIES

A cunning attacker can strike at an unwary opponent from any angle. Sometimes, however, the hunter will become the hunted.

COMBATANTS

This skybattle is fought between 2 flying monsters. Roll off to decide which flying monster will be the Hunter and which will be the Quarry.

SET-UP

Place the Quarry at the centre of the battlefield, facing one edge. Roll a dice for the Hunter and set them up touching the edge of the battlefield, facing towards the Quarry, in the relevant position on the map. The Quarry starts with a velocity of 3. The Hunter can start with any velocity.

VICTORY CONDITIONS

If the Hunter slays the Quarry, the Hunter wins the battle. If the Quarry slays the Hunter or the Hunter leaves the battle and does not return, the Quarry wins the battle. The battle is a draw if the Quarry leaves the battle and does not return.

SKYBATTLE

ENCOUNTER: AIR WAR

Two rival wings approach each other high amongst the clouds. Victory will be claimed by whichever side fights the hardest.

COMBATANTS

This skybattle is fought between 3 or more flying monsters. The players are split into 2 teams that are as evenly matched as possible.

SET-UP

The teams roll off, and the winning team sets up all of their flying monsters first. The teams must set up their flying monsters wholly within their own territory at opposite ends of the battlefield, facing each other, as shown on the map. Choose the starting velocity for each flying monster as it is set up.

VICTORY CONDITIONS

The battle ends when only one team's flying monsters are left on the battlefield. That team wins the battle.

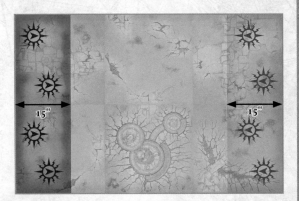

SKYBATTLE

ENCOUNTER: DAWN PATROL

A pack of flying monsters invades enemy territory intent on battle, drawing skybound patrols towards them like moths to the flame.

COMBATANTS

This skybattle is fought between 3 or more flying monsters. The players are split into 2 teams that are as evenly matched as possible. One team is the Invaders. The other team is the Interceptors. If one team has more flying monsters, that team is the Interceptors; otherwise, the teams roll off and the winner chooses which team is the Interceptors.

SET-UP

The Invaders set up their flying monsters first, wholly within 15" of the centre of the battlefield and all facing the same direction, as shown on the map. They start with a velocity of 3.

The Interceptors then set up their flying monsters one by one at alternate ends of the battlefield, wholly within

their territory. Choose the starting velocity for each flying monster as it is set up.

VICTORY CONDITIONS

The battle ends when only one team's flying monsters are left on the battlefield. That team wins the battle.

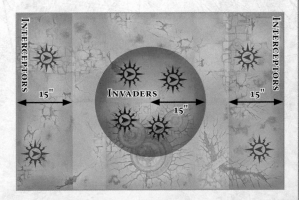

To the north of Thondia, deep in the hinterlands of Ghur, lies the mountain range known as the Gryphspine. Atop a shelf of jagged rock stands the free city of Skythane. Isolated and wracked by the freezing winds, Skythane would likely have been reduced to ruin long ago were it not for the mineral wealth in the surrounding peaks and the skill of its aerial hosts. Great enchanted sky-barques and Kharadron trader-vessels carry this bounty to the southern cities of Izalend and Excelsis. Proud Griffon riders of the Freeguilds and duardin sky-ships accompany these convoys, their blades and guns forever kept at the ready.

And well they should be. Danger lurks amidst the peaks and valleys of the Gryphspine, and many of these threats come on swift wings of their own. Orruks prowl the hinterlands while their ironclad bosses ride huge Maw-krushas, eager to smash anyone they encounter. Nestled in the mountains is the crumbling fortress of Drakshaunt, home to an order of Soulblight vampires who, having become inured over long centuries to the realm's many terrestrial predators, raise up rotten undead beasts upon which to ride. Just as dangerous are the Flesh-eater Courts who lurk

in the caves around Drakshaunt. These degenerate cannibals believe themselves to be the last true defenders of the Gryphspine and are convinced that their cadaverous mounts are the noble silver-furred creatures from which the mountains take their name.

Perhaps most insidious is the taint of Chaos. Chimeras, Manticores and fouler creatures besides haunt the upper altitudes, standing guard over long-lost relics and priceless realmstone deposits. Most of Skythane's citizens dare not risk the peaks, but the Kharadron – stubborn at the best of times and ever hungry for profit – are another matter. Chartered vessels will occasionally brave these dangers, their crews searching for fortune. In doing so, they risk drawing the attention of powerful daemonic entities that feed upon the aetheric currents. The Blood God's children in particular delight in wrecking any skyvessels they come across. A duel between these two powers is akin to an unstoppable force striking against an immovable object – the Kharadron must navigate the gale-wracked skies carefully and keep watch for approaching foes, trusting in their guns to ward off enemies emerging from the storm and give themselves enough time to extract their prize.

SKYBATTLE

ABOVE THE GRYPHSPINE

COMBATANTS

This skybattle is fought between 1 or more Kharadron skyvessels (of any type) and an equal number of Bloodthirsters (of any type). The players are split into 2 teams: the Kharadron Skyvessels team and the Bloodthirsters team.

SET-UP

The teams roll off, and the winning team sets up all of their flying monsters first. The teams must set up their flying monsters wholly within their own territory at opposite ends of the battlefield, facing each other, as shown on the map. Choose the starting velocity for each flying monster as it is set up.

SPECIAL RULES

Gryphspine Peak: Roll a dice before either team sets up and place it at the centre of the battlefield. The dice represents a Gryphspine mountain peak. It is treated as a piece of floating terrain that has a radius equal to the number rolled on the dice, measured from the centre of the dice.

Gale-wracked Skies: At the start of each turn, before the first impulse begins, the Bloodthirsters team must roll 1

dice for each Kharadron skyvessel on the battlefield. On a 6, that Kharadron skyvessel suffers 1 wound.

VICTORY CONDITIONS

If a Kharadron skyvessel ends an impulse within 3" of the Gryphspine peak, then leaves the battle and does not return, the Kharadron Skyvessels team wins the battle. If the only flying monsters left on the battlefield are Bloodthirsters and the Kharadron Skyvessels team has not won, then the Bloodthirsters team wins the battle.

SKIES OF SLAUGHTER CAMPAIGNS

The most exciting way to play Skies of Slaughter is as a campaign. In a campaign, you will be able to track the exploits of your flying monster over the course of several engagements, watching them grow from a fledgling fighter to a legendary veteran!

Any number of players can take part in a campaign, and new players can join in whenever they wish. Campaign battles are fought just like any other battle, except that after each skybattle, the players record information about each of their flying monsters on a notecard, including how many battles they have taken part in, how many kills they have scored and any Veteran Abilities they have learnt.

LONE WOLVES AND WINGS

Each player can either command a single flying monster in a campaign (called a **lone wolf**) or a whole wing. If they decide to command a wing, then each flying monster in the wing must be represented by a different flying monster from the player's collection. This means that a player can start out as a lone wolf, move on to command a wing of 2 or 3 flying monsters, and finally lead a full wing of 4 or more flying monsters!

Lone Wolf: A player using a single flying monster in a campaign is a lone wolf. They will use the same flying monster in every skybattle.

Wing: A player with more than 1 flying monster commands a wing. Up to 3 of the flying monsters in the wing can be fielded in a skybattle.

STARTING EXPERIENCE

All flying monsters start off as fledgling fighters. They will gain experience and learn new skills as they fight campaign battles.

NEW RECRUITS

A player can add flying monsters to their roster at any time. Any new flying monsters start off as fledgling fighters.

SKILL POINTS AND VETERAN ABILITIES

Flying monsters earn Skill Points and Veteran Abilities by taking part in campaign battles and by scoring kills respectively. Players should record the number of battles fought and number of kills scored on their flying monster's notecard.

SKILL POINTS

Flying monsters that have taken part in 1 or more campaign battles receive Skill Points. In a skybattle, the controlling player can use 1 Skill Point to:

- Re-roll 1 hit roll, 1 danger roll, 1 acceleration roll, 1 braking roll, 1 recovery roll or 1 survival roll made for their flying monster.

- Allow their flying monster to make 1 extra Move or 1 extra Turn during 1 manoeuvre.

- Halve the damage inflicted on their flying monster from 1 attack (rounding up).

At the start of each skybattle, look up the number of campaign battles the flying monster has taken part in on the Experience Table to determine how many Skill Points it has for that battle.

EXPERIENCE TABLE	
0 battles	**Fledgling:** 0 Skill Points
1-5 battles	**Experienced:** 1 Skill Point
6+ battles	**Veteran:** 2 Skill Points

Any unused Skill Points are lost at the end of the battle – they cannot be 'saved up' for use in future campaign battles.

VETERAN ABILITIES

A flying monster scores a **kill** if it slays an enemy flying monster or if it is the last flying monster to attack an enemy flying monster before that flying monster spins into the ground and is slain.

At the end of each skybattle, look up the total number of kills the flying monster has scored on the Kill Table to determine the total number of Veteran Abilities it has learnt.

KILL TABLE	
1-2 kills	**Killer:** 1 Veteran Ability
3-4 kills	**Deadly:** 2 Veteran Abilities
5-9 kills	**Notorious:** 3 Veteran Abilities
10-14 kills	**Infamous:** 4 Veteran Abilities
15+ kills	**Legendary:** 5 Veteran Abilities

Roll a **D66** on the Veteran Abilities Table opposite each time a flying monster learns a new Veteran Ability. To do so, roll 2 dice: the first indicates the tens, the second indicates the units. Record the flying monster's abilities on its notecard. Re-roll the result if the flying monster already has that ability.

LORD OF THE SKIES

The flying monster with the most kills at the start of a skybattle is crowned Lord of the Skies and receives 1 extra Skill Point to use during the skybattle. A flying monster must have at least 1 kill to be crowned Lord of the Skies. If several flying monsters are tied with 1 or more kills, then the one that was first to achieve the highest score is crowned Lord of the Skies.

SURVIVAL

If a flying monster is slain in a campaign battle, its death is not assumed to be a certainty: the controlling player must make a **survival roll** on the Survival Table to see if it was truly killed, if it was merely injured or if it managed to escape unharmed. Make a separate survival roll for each flying monster that was slain.

SURVIVAL TABLE

D6	Result
1	Killed
2-3	Injured
4-6	Unharmed

Killed: The flying monster is dead. A new, inexperienced flying monster takes their place.

Injured: An injured flying monster is allowed to take part in a skybattle but cannot use any Skill Points during the battle.

Flying monsters recover from their injuries after they have fought their next skybattle. If the flying monster is part of a wing, it recovers from its injuries after its wing has fought its next skybattle, whether or not the injured flying monster took part in that battle.

Unharmed: The flying monster is back to full strength and ready for battle!

VETERAN ABILITIES TABLE

D66	Result
11-12	**Cool-headed:** You can choose to roll 1, 2 or 3 dice when making an initiative roll for this flying monster or the wing it is part of.
13-14	**Lucky:** This flying monster receives 1 extra Skill Point at the start of each skybattle.
15-16	**Speed Merchant:** You can re-roll acceleration rolls of 6 or less for this flying monster, and it can make 1 extra Move when performing a Level Flight manoeuvre.
21-22	**Skilled Flyer:** You can re-roll failed danger rolls for this flying monster.
23-24	**Crack Shot:** You can re-roll hit rolls of 1 for this flying monster.
25-26	**Eagle-eyed:** Add 5" to the range of each of this flying monster's weapons.
31-32	**Killer Instincts:** When rolling on the Damage Table for this flying monster, you can add or subtract 1 from the roll.
33-34	**Find Weaknesses:** When this flying monster makes an attack, reduce the target's Toughness characteristic by 1.
35-36	**Slippery:** Opponents must re-roll hit rolls of 6.
41-42	**Signature Move:** Pick a manoeuvre on this flying monster's warscroll. This flying monster will perform that manoeuvre safely at all velocities on a 2+.
43-44	**Born Leader:** At the start of a skybattle, you can give 1 or more of your Skill Points to other flying monsters on your team.
45-46	**Lightning Turns:** When this flying monster performs a manoeuvre, 1 of its Turns can be up to 90 degrees instead of up to 45 degrees.
51-52	**Hunter:** This flying monster counts as tailing if it is in its target's Rear 180° weapon arc instead of its Rear 90° weapon arc.
53-54	**Honed Reactions:** When this flying monster retaliates, do not subtract 1 from hit rolls.
55-56	**Born Survivor:** You can re-roll recovery rolls, collision rolls and survival rolls of 1 for this flying monster.
61-66	**Choose:** You can choose which ability this flying monster learns.

VELOCITY 4
WOUNDS 5
RECOVERY 8+
TOUGHNESS 5

24

LORD-CELESTANT
ON STARDRAKE

Only the mightiest and noblest souls are chosen to lead an Extremis Chamber. The Lord-Celestant and his steed are so infused with celestial power that they radiate azure energies. The power of the stars themselves is theirs to command.

WEAPON	Arc	Range	Hit Rolls	Damage	Strafe
Celestine Hammer	360°	3"	3+ 3+ 3+	2	+1
Stormbound Blade	360°	3"	3+ 3+ 3+	D3	+1
Great Claws	Forward 90°	3"	4+ 4+ 4+	2	+2

WEAPONS

Celestine Hammer and Great Claws. The Celestine Hammer can be replaced with a *Stormbound Blade*.

SPECIAL RULES

Lord of the Heavens: When this model attacks, instead of attacking with its weapons, you can pick up to D6 different enemy flying monsters and roll a dice for each model. On a 4+, that model suffers 2 wounds.

MANOEUVRE TABLE				
Manoeuvre	**Velocity**			**Execution**
	2	3	4	
Level Flight	Always Safe			Move Move
Swerve	2+	3+	4+	Move Sideslip Move
Bank	2+	3+	4+	Move Move Turn
Turn	3+	4+	5+	Move Turn Move
Snap Turn	4+	5+	6+	Turn Move Move
Stoop	4+	5+	6+	Move Turn OR Turn Move

VELOCITY 4
WOUNDS 5
RECOVERY 8+
TOUGHNESS 5

DRAKESWORN TEMPLAR

Drakesworn Templars are the heavens' might made manifest. They ride immense Stardrakes that can roar forth lightning-charged clouds, summon starfire from the skies around them or rip through steel and flesh alike with their sharp claws.

WEAPON	Arc	Range	Hit Rolls	Damage	Strafe
Skybolt Bow	Forward 180°	15"	4+	D3	+1
Tempest Axe	360°	3"	4+ 4+ 4+	2	+1
Arc Hammer	Forward 180°	3"	4+ 4+	3	+1
Stormlance	Forward 90°	3"	4+ 4+ 4+	2	+2
Great Claws	Forward 180°	3"	3+ 3+ 3+	2	0

WEAPONS

Tempest Axe and Great Claws. The Tempest Axe can be replaced with an *Arc Hammer* or *Stormlance*. The model can also wield a *Skybolt Bow*, but if it does, roll 1 fewer dice when attacking with its Tempest Axe, Arc Hammer or Stormlance.

MANOEUVRE TABLE				
Manoeuvre	**Velocity**			**Execution**
	2	3	4	
Level Flight	Always Safe			Move Move
Swerve	2+	3+	4+	Move Sideslip Move
Bank	2+	3+	4+	Move Move Turn
Turn	3+	4+	5+	Move Turn Move
Snap Turn	4+	5+	6+	Turn Move Move
Stoop	4+	5+	6+	Move Turn OR Turn Move

SPECIAL RULES

Lord of the Heavens: When this model attacks, instead of attacking with its weapons, you can pick up to D6 different enemy flying monsters and roll a dice for each model. On a 4+, that model suffers 2 wounds.

● SKIES OF SLAUGHTER WARSCROLL ●

BATTLEMAGE
ON GRIFFON

Velocity 5 / Wounds 4 / Recovery 9+ / Toughness 3

When mounted atop a furious, twin-headed Ghurish Griffon, an Amber Battlemage can lay waste to their foes from afar or strike from on high in a vicious frenzy of stabbing beaks and ripping talons.

WEAPON	Arc	Range	Hit Rolls	Damage	Strafe
Amber Spear Spell	Forward 180°	12"	4+	D6	+1
Beaststaff	360°	3"	5+	D3	0
Razor Claws	Forward 180°	3"	4+ 4+ 4+ 4+	2	+2
Twin Beaks	Forward 90°	3"	4+ 4+ 4+ 4+	1	0

WEAPONS

Amber Spear Spell, Beaststaff, Razor Claws and Twin Beaks.

SPECIAL RULES

Mystic Shield: Instead of making a Spell attack, this model can cast Mystic Shield on itself. If it does so, add 1 to this model's Toughness characteristic until the start of its next action.

MANOEUVRE TABLE					
Manoeuvre	Velocity				Execution
	2	3	4	5	
Level Flight	Always Safe				Move Move
Swerve	2+	2+	3+	4+	Move Sideslip Move
Bank	2+	3+	4+	5+	Move Move Turn
Turn	3+	4+	5+	6+	Move Turn Move
Snap Turn	4+	5+	6+	7+	Turn Move Move
Stoop	4+	5+	6+	7+	Move Turn OR Turn Move
Wing Over	5+	6+	7+	8+	Move Reverse Move

● SKIES OF SLAUGHTER WARSCROLL ●

FREEGUILD GENERAL
ON GRIFFON

Velocity 5 / Wounds 4 / Recovery 9+ / Toughness 4

A Freeguild General mounted upon a noble griffon surveys the battlefield from on high. Identifying where their presence is most required, they descend like a speeding comet to lay waste to their enemies, inspiring their comrades with word and deed.

WEAPON	Arc	Range	Hit Rolls	Damage	Strafe
Sigmarite Runesword	360°	3"	4+ 4+ 4+ 4+	2	+1
Sigmarite Greathammer	Forward 180°	3"	4+ 4+ 4+	3	+1
Freeguild Lance	Forward 90°	3"	3+ 3+ 3+	D3	+2
Razor Claws	Forward 180°	3"	4+ 4+ 4+ 4+	2	+2
Deadly Beak	Forward 90°	3"	4+ 4+	2	0

WEAPONS

Sigmarite Runesword, Razor Claws and Deadly Beak. The Sigmarite Runesword can be replaced with a *Sigmarite Greathammer* or *Freeguild Lance*.

SPECIAL RULES

Rousing Battle Cry: Add 1 to recovery rolls for this model and all friendly flying monsters within 12" of this model.

MANOEUVRE TABLE					
Manoeuvre	Velocity				Execution
	2	3	4	5	
Level Flight	Always Safe				Move Move
Swerve	2+	2+	3+	4+	Move Sideslip Move
Bank	2+	3+	4+	5+	Move Move Turn
Turn	3+	4+	5+	6+	Move Turn Move
Snap Turn	4+	5+	6+	7+	Turn Move Move
Stoop	4+	5+	6+	7+	Move Turn OR Turn Move
Wing Over	5+	6+	7+	8+	Move Reverse Move

VELOCITY 4
TOUGHNESS 3
WOUNDS 5
RECOVERY 9+

SORCERESS
ON BLACK DRAGON

Many Sorceresses go to war upon fearsome Black Dragons, delighting in the terror in the eyes of their enemies as the scaled beasts spit clouds of choking black fumes and rip their prey apart with sword-sized talons.

WEAPON	Arc	Range	Hit Rolls	Damage	Strafe
Bladewind Spell	Forward 180°	12"	5+ 5+ 5+	1	+2
Witch Rod	360°	3"	5+	D3	0
Darkling Sword	360°	3"	4+ 4+	1	0
Razor-sharp Claws	Forward 90°	3"	5+ 5+ 5+ 5+	2	+1
Fearsome Jaws	Forward 180°	3"	5+ 5+ 5+	D6	0

WEAPONS

Bladewind Spell, Witch Rod, Razor-sharp Claws and Fearsome Jaws.
The Witch Rod can be replaced with a *Darkling Sword*.

SPECIAL RULES

Noxious Breath: When this model attacks a ground target, the controlling player can roll 3D6 instead of 2D6 and pick which 2 dice to use for the ground attack roll.

MANOEUVRE TABLE

Manoeuvre	Velocity			Execution
	2	3	4	
Level Flight	Always Safe			Move Move
Swerve	2+	3+	4+	Move Sideslip Move
Bank	2+	3+	4+	Move Move Turn
Turn	3+	4+	5+	Move Turn Move
Snap Turn	4+	5+	6+	Turn Move Move
Stoop	4+	5+	6+	Move Turn OR Turn Move
Circle Back	5+	6+	7+	Turn Move Turn

Mystic Shield: Instead of making a Spell attack, this model can cast Mystic Shield on itself. If it does so, add 1 to this model's Toughness characteristic until the start of its next action.

VELOCITY 4
TOUGHNESS 4
WOUNDS 5
RECOVERY 9+

DREADLORD
ON BLACK DRAGON

The feared warlords of the Order Serpentis delight in inflicting pain and terror upon their foes. They ride to war on obsidian-scaled dragons that can lay waste to entire armies with their dagger-like claws and foul, choking breath.

WEAPON	Arc	Range	Hit Rolls	Damage	Strafe
Exile Blade	360°	3"	4+ 4+ 4+ 4+ 4+	1	+1
Lance of Spite	Forward 90°	3"	3+ 3+ 3+	D3	+1
Repeater Crossbow	Forward 180°	3"	4+ 4+	1	+1
Razor-sharp Claws	Forward 90°	3"	5+ 5+ 5+ 5+	2	+1
Fearsome Jaws	Forward 180°	3"	5+ 5+ 5+	D6	0

WEAPONS

Exile Blade, Repeater Crossbow, Razor-sharp Claws and Fearsome Jaws. The Exile Blade can be replaced with a *Lance of Spite*. The Repeater Crossbow can be replaced with a *Tyrant's Shield*.

SPECIAL RULES

Noxious Breath: When this model attacks a ground target, the controlling player can roll 3D6 instead of 2D6 and pick which 2 dice to use for the ground attack roll.

MANOEUVRE TABLE

Manoeuvre	Velocity			Execution
	2	3	4	
Level Flight	Always Safe			Move Move
Swerve	2+	3+	4+	Move Sideslip Move
Bank	2+	3+	4+	Move Move Turn
Turn	3+	4+	5+	Move Turn Move
Snap Turn	4+	5+	6+	Turn Move Move
Stoop	4+	5+	6+	Move Turn OR Turn Move
Circle Back	5+	6+	7+	Turn Move Turn

Tyrant's Shield: If this model has a Tyrant's Shield, when this model is attacked, subtract 1 from the total damage inflicted before looking up the result on the Attack Results Table.

AKHELIAN LEVIADON

A hulking monster, the Akhelian Leviadon is clad in thick scales and protected by a hardened shell. It bears an impressive crew, including a pair of harpoon launcher operators and a musician whose void drum sends forth arcane reverberations.

WEAPON	Arc	Range	Hit Rolls	Damage	Strafe
Razorshell Harpoon Launchers	Forward 180°	15"	4+ 4+ 4+ 4+	2	+3
Twin-pronged Spear	360°	3"	4+ 4+	2	+1
Crushing Jaws	Forward 90°	3"	3+	D6	0
Massive Scythed Fins	Forward 180°	3"	4+ 4+ 4+ 4+	2	+2

WEAPONS

Razorshell Harpoon Launchers, Twin-pronged Spear, Crushing Jaws and Massive Scythed Fins.

SPECIAL RULES

Cumbersome: Subtract 2 from acceleration and braking rolls for this model.

Void Drum: Enemy flying monsters do not receive a bonus to their hit rolls for tailing this model.

MANOEUVRE TABLE			
Manoeuvre	Velocity		Execution
	2	3	
Level Flight	Always Safe		Move Move
Swerve	3+	5+	Move Sideslip Move
Bank	3+	5+	Move Move Turn
Turn	4+	6+	Move Turn Move
Stoop	5+	7+	Move Turn OR Turn Move

AKHELIAN ALLOPEX

Allopexes are vicious predators, known for their voracious appetites and savage blood frenzies. As Akhelian bond-beasts, they are more dangerous still – even the bravest fear to see these finned menaces approach.

WEAPON	Arc	Range	Hit Rolls	Damage	Strafe
Razorshell Harpoon Launcher	Forward 180°	12"	4+ 4+	2	+1
Retarius Net Launcher	Forward 180°	12"	3+	3	+2
Barbed Hooks and Blades	360°	3"	5+ 5+ 5+ 5+ 5+	1	+1
Ferocious Bites	Forward 90°	3"	4+	3	+1
Scythed Fins	Forward 180°	3"	4+ 4+ 4+ 4+	1	+1

WEAPONS

Razorshell Harpoon Launcher, Barbed Hooks and Blades, Ferocious Bites, and Scythed Fins. The Razorshell Harpoon Launcher can be replaced with a *Retarius Net Launcher*.

SPECIAL RULES

Bloodthirsty Predator: Add 2 to acceleration and braking rolls for this model.

MANOEUVRE TABLE					
Manoeuvre	Velocity				Execution
	2	3	4	5	
Level Flight	Always Safe				Move Move
Swerve	2+	3+	4+	4+	Move Sideslip Move
Bank	2+	3+	4+	5+	Move Move Turn
Turn	2+	3+	4+	5+	Move Turn Move
Snap Turn	3+	4+	5+	5+	Turn Move Move
Circle Back	3+	4+	5+	6+	Turn Move Turn
Rear Round	4+	5+	6+	6+	Reverse Move OR Move Reverse

28

VELOCITY **5**
TOUGHNESS **4**
WOUNDS **4**
RECOVERY **7+**

FROSTHEART PHOENIX

Some of the Ur-Phoenix's spawn radiate the elemental power of ice. Surrounded by a freezing aura that slows nearby foes to a crawl, these Frostheart Phoenixes strike from on high with deadly force, ripping and tearing their prey to pieces.

WEAPON	Arc	Range	Hit Rolls	Damage	Strafe
Ice-cold Talons	Forward 180°	3"	4+ 4+ 4+ 4+ 4+	2	+2

WEAPONS

Ice-cold Talons.

SPECIAL RULES

Blizzard Aura: Subtract 1 from hit rolls for attacks made by enemy models within 3" of this model.

Swift: Add 2 to acceleration and braking rolls for this model.

MANOEUVRE TABLE					
Manoeuvre	Velocity				Execution
	2	3	4	5	
Level Flight	Always Safe				Move Move
Bank	2+	2+	3+	4+	Move Move Turn
Swerve	2+	2+	3+	4+	Move Sideslip Move
Turn	2+	3+	4+	5+	Move Turn Move
Snap Turn	3+	4+	5+	6+	Turn Move Move
Wing Over	4+	5+	6+	7+	Move Reverse Move

VELOCITY **5**
TOUGHNESS **4**
WOUNDS **4**
RECOVERY **4+**

FLAMESPYRE PHOENIX

Trailing blazing streams of fire, Flamespyre Phoenixes sweep low over the heads of their prey, engulfing them in a magical inferno. Even if brought low by blade or spell, these creatures are reborn in a blinding burst of light and heat.

WEAPON	Arc	Range	Hit Rolls	Damage	Strafe
Flaming Talons	Forward 180°	3"	4+ 4+ 4+ 4+	2	+2
Wake of Fire	Rear 90°	3"	4+	D6	0

WEAPONS

Flaming Talons and Wake of Fire.

SPECIAL RULES

Swift: Add 2 to acceleration and braking rolls for this model.

Wake of Fire: Enemy flying monsters do not receive a bonus to their hit rolls for tailing this model.

MANOEUVRE TABLE					
Manoeuvre	Velocity				Execution
	2	3	4	5	
Level Flight	Always Safe				Move Move
Bank	2+	2+	3+	4+	Move Move Turn
Swerve	2+	2+	3+	4+	Move Sideslip Move
Turn	2+	3+	4+	5+	Move Turn Move
Snap Turn	3+	4+	5+	6+	Turn Move Move
Wing Over	4+	5+	6+	7+	Move Reverse Move

VELOCITY
4
TOUGHNESS 4 X 5 WOUNDS
7+
RECOVERY

ANOINTED
ON FROSTHEART PHOENIX

Elder Anointed may choose to ride to battle atop a Frostheart Phoenix, finding a kindred spirit in these patient and deliberate beings. From them radiates an elemental aura of numbing cold that can freeze a foe near solid.

WEAPON	Arc	Range	Hit Rolls	Damage	Strafe
Ice-cold Talons	Forward 180°	3"	4+ 4+ 4+ 4+ 4+	2	+2
Great Phoenix Halberd	360°	3"	4+ 4+ 4+ 4+	1	+1

WEAPONS

Ice-cold Talons and Great Phoenix Halberd.

SPECIAL RULES

Blizzard Aura: Subtract 1 from hit rolls for attacks made by enemy models within 3" of this model.

MANOEUVRE TABLE				
Manoeuvre	**Velocity**			**Execution**
	2	3	4	
Level Flight	Always Safe			Move Move
Bank	2+	2+	3+	Move Move Turn
Swerve	2+	2+	3+	Move Sideslip Move
Turn	2+	3+	4+	Move Turn Move
Snap Turn	3+	4+	5+	Turn Move Move

VELOCITY
4
TOUGHNESS 4 X 5 WOUNDS
4+
RECOVERY

ANOINTED
ON FLAMESPYRE PHOENIX

Those Anointed whose fates lead them into the most furious conflicts often form a close bond with a Flamespyre Phoenix. In battle, the blazing power of this majestic creature and the skill of their aelven ally make for a potent combination.

WEAPON	Arc	Range	Hit Rolls	Damage	Strafe
Flaming Talons	Forward 180°	3"	4+ 4+ 4+ 4+	2	+2
Great Phoenix Halberd	360°	3"	4+ 4+ 4+ 4+	1	+1
Wake of Fire	Rear 90°	3"	4+	D6	0

WEAPONS

Flaming Talons, Great Phoenix Halberd and Wake of Fire.

SPECIAL RULES

Wake of Fire: Enemy flying monsters do not receive a bonus to their hit rolls for tailing this model.

MANOEUVRE TABLE				
Manoeuvre	**Velocity**			**Execution**
	2	3	4	
Level Flight	Always Safe			Move Move
Bank	2+	2+	3+	Move Move Turn
Swerve	2+	2+	3+	Move Sideslip Move
Turn	2+	3+	4+	Move Turn Move
Snap Turn	3+	4+	5+	Turn Move Move

ARKANAUT IRONCLAD

Amongst the heaviest Kharadron ships of the line, the redoubtable Ironclads provide a floating fortress of iron at the heart of any airfleet, bombarding their targets from afar with explosive missiles and armour-piercing torpedoes.

WEAPON	Arc	Range	Hit Rolls	Damage	Strafe
Great Sky Cannon	Forward 180°	18"	4+ 4+ 4+	4	+2
Great Skyhook	Forward 180°	18"	3+	2D6	0
Great Volley Cannon	Forward 180°	12"	2+ 2+ 2+ 2+	2	+3
Aethershock Torpedoes	Fixed	15"	5+ 5+ 5+ 5+	D3	0
Aethershot Carbines	Forward 180°	9"	4+ 4+ 4+ 4+	2	+1
Boarding Weapons	360°	3"	5+ 5+ 5+ 5+ 5+	1	0

WEAPONS

Great Sky Cannon, Aethershock Torpedoes, Aethershot Carbines and Boarding Weapons.
The Great Sky Cannon can be replaced with a *Great Skyhook* or *Great Volley Cannon*.

SPECIAL RULES

Cumbersome: Subtract 2 from acceleration and braking rolls for this model.

MANOEUVRE TABLE			
Manoeuvre	**Velocity**		**Execution**
	2	3	
Level Flight	Always Safe		Move Move
Swerve	2+	5+	Move Sideslip Move
Bank	2+	5+	Move Move Turn
Turn	3+	7+	Move Turn Move

ARKANAUT FRIGATE

The sleek and deadly profile of an Arkanaut Frigate is a sight greatly feared by the Kharadron's many enemies, who know all too well the devastating firepower these airships possess and the fighting spirit of the privateers they carry into battle.

WEAPON	Arc	Range	Hit Rolls	Damage	Strafe
Heavy Sky Cannon	Forward 180°	15"	4+ 4+ 4+	2	+1
Heavy Skyhook	Forward 180°	15"	3+	D6	0
Aethershot Carbines	Forward 180°	9"	4+ 4+	2	+1
Boarding Weapons	360°	3"	5+ 5+ 5+	1	0

WEAPONS

Heavy Sky Cannon, Aethershot Carbines and Boarding Weapons.
The Heavy Sky Cannon can be replaced with a *Heavy Skyhook*.

SPECIAL RULES

Bomb Racks: If this model completes a manoeuvre and has passed over an enemy flying monster, roll a dice. On a 4+, that enemy flying monster suffers 1 wound.

MANOEUVRE TABLE				
Manoeuvre	**Velocity**			**Execution**
	2	3	4	
Level Flight	Always Safe			Move Move
Ahead Slow	Always Safe			Move Turn
Ahead Full	4+	3+	2+	Move Move Move
Swerve	2+	3+	4+	Move Sideslip Move
Bank	2+	3+	4+	Move Move Turn
Turn	3+	4+	5+	Move Turn Move
Circle About	4+	5+	6+	Turn Move Turn

VELOCITY 5
TOUGHNESS 4 — 3 WOUNDS
9+ RECOVERY

GRUNDSTOK GUNHAULER

Small, manoeuvrable and deadly, the Grundstok Gunhauler is an escort-class ship tasked with ensuring the safety of the airfleets' larger skyvessels. They perform this role well, swarming in defence before peeling off to launch deadly attack runs.

WEAPON	Arc	Range	Hit Rolls	Damage	Strafe
Sky Cannon	Forward 180°	12"	4+ 4+ 4+	2	+1
Drill Cannon	Forward 180°	24"	3+	D3	0
Aethershot Carbine	Forward 180°	9"	5+ 5+	1	+1
Boarding Weapons	360°	3"	5+ 5+ 5+	1	0

WEAPONS

Sky Cannon, Aethershot Carbine and Boarding Weapons.
The Sky Cannon can be replaced with a *Drill Cannon*.

SPECIAL RULES

Bomb Racks: If this model completes a manoeuvre and has passed over an enemy flying monster, roll a dice. On a 5+, that enemy flying monster suffers 1 wound.

Manoeuvre	Velocity				Execution
	2	3	4	5	
Level Flight	Always Safe				Move Move
Ahead Slow	Always Safe				Move Turn
Ahead Full	4+	3+	2+	Safe	Move Move Move
Swerve	Safe	2+	3+	4+	Move Sideslip Move
Bank	Safe	2+	3+	4+	Move Move Turn
Turn	2+	3+	4+	5+	Move Turn Move
Hard Turn	2+	3+	4+	5+	Turn Move Move
Hard About	3+	4+	5+	6+	Move Reverse Move

VELOCITY 4
TOUGHNESS 4 — 5 WOUNDS
7+ RECOVERY

WRATH OF KHORNE

BLOODTHIRSTER

Wrath of Khorne Bloodthirsters are the Lord of Battle's agents of vengeance, sent to claim the skulls of those who have offended him. With hellforged weapons and breath of purest hellfire, they lay low their quarry, slicing and melting flesh from bone.

WEAPON	Arc	Range	Hit Rolls	Damage	Strafe
Hellfire Breath	Forward 90°	7"	2+	D3	+2
Bloodflail	Forward 90°	9"	4+	2	+2
Mighty Axe of Khorne	Forward 180°	3"	4+ 4+ 4+ 4+	D3	+2

WEAPONS

Hellfire Breath, Bloodflail and Mighty Axe of Khorne.

SPECIAL RULES

Rune-crown of Khorne: Subtract 1 from hit rolls for Spell attacks made by enemy models within 18" of this model.

Manoeuvre	Velocity			Execution
	2	3	4	
Level Flight	Always Safe			Move Move
Charge	4+	3+	2+	Move Move Move
Swerve	2+	3+	4+	Move Sideslip Move
Bank	2+	3+	4+	Move Move Turn
Turn	3+	4+	5+	Move Turn Move
Snap Turn	4+	5+	6+	Turn Move Move
Circle Back	5+	6+	7+	Turn Move Turn

BLOODTHIRSTER
OF INSENSATE RAGE

Those Bloodthirsters that wield colossal Great Axes of Khorne are particularly feared by the denizens of the realms who ply the airways, for they can send even the mightiest flying combatants tumbling groundwards in a deluge of wreckage and gore.

WEAPON	Arc	Range	Hit Rolls	Damage	Strafe
Great Axe of Khorne	Forward 180°	3"	4+ 4+ 4+ 4+	D6	+4

WEAPONS

Great Axe of Khorne.

SPECIAL RULES

Rage Unbound: Add 1 to hit rolls for attacks made by this model if the last manoeuvre it performed was a Bloodthirsty Charge. This bonus does not apply to retaliation attacks.

MANOEUVRE TABLE				
Manoeuvre	**Velocity**			**Execution**
	2	3	4	
Level Flight	Always Safe			Move Move
Bloodthirsty Charge	Always Safe			Move Move Move
Swerve	2+	3+	4+	Move Sideslip Move
Bank	2+	3+	4+	Move Move Turn
Turn	3+	4+	5+	Move Turn Move
Snap Turn	4+	5+	6+	Turn Move Move
Circle Back	5+	6+	7+	Turn Move Turn

BLOODTHIRSTER
OF UNFETTERED FURY

Descending from the clouds like a crimson comet, the Bloodthirster of Unfettered Fury crashes into its prey, its barbed whip lashing out to rend both iron and flesh, the very air around its hulking form burning in the heat of its rage.

WEAPON	Arc	Range	Hit Rolls	Damage	Strafe
Lash of Khorne	Forward 90°	9"	4+ 4+ 4+	D3	+2
Mighty Axe of Khorne	Forward 180°	3"	4+ 4+ 4+ 4+	D3	+2

WEAPONS

Lash of Khorne and Mighty Axe of Khorne.

SPECIAL RULES

Drawn to the Kill: Subtract 2 from danger rolls for enemy models that are within 3" of this model.

MANOEUVRE TABLE				
Manoeuvre	**Velocity**			**Execution**
	2	3	4	
Level Flight	Always Safe			Move Move
Charge	4+	3+	2+	Move Move Move
Swerve	2+	3+	4+	Move Sideslip Move
Bank	2+	3+	4+	Move Move Turn
Turn	3+	4+	5+	Move Turn Move
Snap Turn	4+	5+	6+	Turn Move Move
Circle Back	5+	6+	7+	Turn Move Turn

LORD OF CHANGE

VELOCITY 4 / WOUNDS 5 / RECOVERY 7+ / TOUGHNESS 4

The greatest of Tzeentch's daemons, the Lords of Change shimmer with raw magic. With a flick of their claw, they can hurl foes into the nightmarish Realm of Chaos, blast enemies with wyrdfire or steal opponents' spells for their own use.

WEAPON	Arc	Range	Hit Rolls	Damage	Strafe
Infernal Gateway Spell	Forward 180°	12"	5+ 5+ 5+	3	+3
Staff of Tzeentch	Forward 180°	3"	4+ 4+ 4+	2	+1
Baleful Sword	Forward 180°	3"	4+ 4+	3	0
Curved Beak and Wicked Talons	Forward 180°	3"	5+ 5+ 5+ 5+	2	0

WEAPONS

Infernal Gateway Spell, Staff of Tzeentch, Baleful Sword, and Curved Beak and Wicked Talons.

SPECIAL RULES

Mystic Shield: Instead of making a Spell attack, this model can cast Mystic Shield on itself. If it does so, add 1 to this model's Toughness characteristic until the start of its next action.

MANOEUVRE TABLE				
Manoeuvre	**Velocity**			**Execution**
	2	3	4	
Level Flight	Always Safe			Move Move
Bank	2+	3+	4+	Move Move Turn
Turn	3+	4+	5+	Move Turn Move
Snap Turn	4+	5+	6+	Turn Move Move
Stoop	4+	5+	6+	Move Turn OR Turn Move
Circle Back	5+	6+	7+	Turn Move Turn

DAEMON PRINCE

VELOCITY 4 / WOUNDS 3 / RECOVERY 7+ / TOUGHNESS 5

Those champions who consistently please their patron god may eventually be granted immortality as a Daemon Prince. Each of these black-hearted monsters is a living icon of their master's power and a terrifying foe to face in battle.

WEAPON	Arc	Range	Hit Rolls	Damage	Strafe
Daemonic Axe	Forward 180°	3"	4+ 4+ 4+	2	+2
Hellforged Sword	Forward 180°	3"	5+ 5+ 5+	3	+2
Malefic Talons	Forward 180°	3"	4+ 4+ 4+ 4+ 4+	1	+1

WEAPONS

Daemonic Axe and Malefic Talons. The Daemonic Axe can be replaced with a *Hellforged Sword*.

SPECIAL RULES

Immortal Champion: This model can carry out retaliation attacks after it has been chosen to be the target of an enemy attack but before the enemy model's attack has been resolved.

MANOEUVRE TABLE				
Manoeuvre	**Velocity**			**Execution**
	2	3	4	
Level Flight	Always Safe			Move Move
Swerve	Always Safe			Move Sideslip Move
Bank	Always Safe			Move Move Turn
Turn	Safe	2+	3+	Move Turn Move
Snap Turn	2+	3+	4+	Turn Move Move
Circle Back	3+	4+	5+	Turn Move Turn
Rear Round	4+	5+	6+	Reverse Move OR Move Reverse

CHAOS SORCERER LORD
ON MANTICORE

VELOCITY
4
TOUGHNESS 4 — 4 WOUNDS
9+
RECOVERY

The binding magic of a Sorcerer Lord can break the will of even a mighty Manticore. Upon such a mount, they plunge headlong into the foe, summoning gales of dark energy as the Manticore tears the enemy asunder.

WEAPON	Arc	Range	Hit Rolls	Damage	Strafe
Wind of Chaos Spell	Forward 180°	12"	4+	D3	+3
Sorcerous Reaping Staff	Forward 180°	3"	4+ 4+ 4+	D3	+1
Honed Fangs and Claws	Forward 180°	3"	4+ 4+ 4+ 4+ 4+	2	+2
Shredding Tail	Rear 180°	3"	5+ 5+ 5+	1	0

WEAPONS

Wind of Chaos Spell, Sorcerous Reaping Staff, Honed Fangs and Claws, and Shredding Tail.

SPECIAL RULES

Mystic Shield: Instead of making a Spell attack, this model can cast Mystic Shield on itself. If it does so, add 1 to this model's Toughness characteristic until the start of its next action.

MANOEUVRE TABLE				
Manoeuvre	Velocity			Execution
	2	3	4	
Level Flight	Always Safe			Move Move
Swerve	2+	3+	4+	Move Sideslip Turn
Bank	2+	3+	4+	Move Move Turn
Turn	3+	4+	5+	Move Turn Move
Snap Turn	4+	5+	6+	Turn Move Move
Stoop	4+	5+	6+	Move Turn OR Turn Move

CHAOS LORD
ON MANTICORE

VELOCITY
4
TOUGHNESS 4 — 4 WOUNDS
9+
RECOVERY

With raw strength and force of will, the greatest Chaos Lords seek to claim a ferocious Manticore as a mount. Those who succeed are amongst the deadliest champions of the Ruinous Powers, their killing power greatly amplified.

WEAPON	Arc	Range	Hit Rolls	Damage	Strafe
Daemon Blade	360°	3"	4+ 4+ 4+	D3	+1
Chaos Lance	Forward 90°	3"	3+ 3+	3	+1
Chaos Flail	Forward 180°	3"	5+ 5+ 5+ 5+ 5+	2	+1
Honed Fangs and Claws	Forward 180°	3"	4+ 4+ 4+ 4+ 4+	2	+2
Shredding Tail	Rear 180°	3"	5+ 5+ 5+	1	0

WEAPONS

Daemon Blade, Chaos Lance, Honed Fangs and Claws, and Shredding Tail.
The Daemon Blade can be replaced with a *Chaos Flail*.
The Chaos Lance can be replaced with a *Chaos Runeshield* or *Daggerfist*.

MANOEUVRE TABLE				
Manoeuvre	Velocity			Execution
	2	3	4	
Level Flight	Always Safe			Move Move
Swerve	2+	3+	4+	Move Sideslip Turn
Bank	2+	3+	4+	Move Move Turn
Turn	3+	4+	5+	Move Turn Move
Snap Turn	4+	5+	6+	Turn Move Move
Stoop	4+	5+	6+	Move Turn OR Turn Move
Circle Back	5+	6+	7+	Turn Move Turn

SPECIAL RULES

Chaos Runeshield or Daggerfist: If this model has a Chaos Runeshield or Daggerfist, it has a Toughness characteristic of 5 instead of 4.

(VELOCITY 4 / WOUNDS 4 / RECOVERY 9+ / TOUGHNESS 3)

CHIMERA

With powerful beats of its great leathery wings, a Chimera soars through the sky. A terrifying mixture of bestial body parts bound together by raw Chaos energy, its three sets of eyes hungrily scan the horizon in search of prey.

WEAPON	Arc	Range	Hit Rolls	Damage	Strafe
Fiery Breath	Forward 90°	10"	2+ 2+	D3	+1
Avian Head	Forward 180°	3"	5+ 5+ 5+	D3	+1
Draconic Head	Forward 180°	3"	5+ 5+ 5+	2	+1
Leonine Head	Forward 180°	3"	3+ 3+ 3+	1	+1
Mauling Claws	Forward 90°	3"	5+ 5+ 5+ 5+ 5+	1	+1

WEAPONS

Fiery Breath, Avian Head, Draconic Head, Leonine Head and Mauling Claws.

SPECIAL RULES

Gouts of Flame: When this model attacks a ground target, the controlling player can roll 3D6 instead of 2D6 and pick which 2 dice to use for the ground attack roll.

MANOEUVRE TABLE				
Manoeuvre	Velocity			Execution
	2	3	4	
Level Flight	Always Safe			Move Move
Swerve	2+	3+	4+	Move Sideslip Turn
Bank	2+	3+	4+	Move Move Turn
Turn	3+	4+	5+	Move Turn Move
Snap Turn	4+	5+	6+	Turn Move Move
Rear Round	4+	5+	6+	Move Reverse OR Reverse Move

Swift: Add 2 to acceleration and braking rolls for this model.

(VELOCITY 4 / WOUNDS 5 / RECOVERY 9+ / TOUGHNESS 4)

ROYAL ZOMBIE DRAGON

With a deafening roar, the Zombie Dragon swoops into battle, eye sockets aglow with necromantic energy. The beast shreds flesh, bone and steel with equal ease, its talons and maw matched in their lethality only by its billowing pestilential breath.

WEAPON	Arc	Range	Hit Rolls	Damage	Strafe
Snapping Maw	Forward 180°	3"	5+ 5+ 5+	D6	+2
Sword-like Claws	Forward 90°	3"	5+ 5+ 5+ 5+ 5+	2	+2

WEAPONS

Snapping Maw and Sword-like Claws.

SPECIAL RULES

Pestilential Breath: When this model attacks a ground target, the controlling player can roll 3D6 instead of 2D6 and pick which 2 dice to use for the ground attack roll.

MANOEUVRE TABLE				
Manoeuvre	Velocity			Execution
	2	3	4	
Level Flight	Always Safe			Move Move
Swerve	2+	3+	4+	Move Sideslip Move
Bank	2+	3+	4+	Move Move Turn
Turn	3+	4+	5+	Move Turn Move
Snap Turn	4+	5+	6+	Turn Move Move
Stoop	4+	5+	6+	Move Turn OR Turn Move
Circle Back	5+	6+	7+	Turn Move Turn

ABHORRANT GHOUL KING
ON ROYAL ZOMBIE DRAGON

VELOCITY 4
WOUNDS 5
RECOVERY 7+
TOUGHNESS 4

Surrounded by an aura of potent dark magic, the Abhorrant Ghoul King and his Zombie Dragon are death incarnate. The sky shudders to the beat of leathery wings as the monster spews forth a coiling cloud of killing miasma.

WEAPON	Arc	Range	Hit Rolls	Damage	Strafe
Arcane Bolt Spell	Forward 180°	12"	4+	D3	+1
Gory Talons and Fangs	360°	3"	5+ 5+ 5+ 5+ 5+	1	+1
Snapping Maw	Forward 180°	3"	5+ 5+ 5+	D6	+2
Sword-like Claws	Forward 90°	3"	5+ 5+ 5+ 5+ 5+	2	+2

WEAPONS

Arcane Bolt Spell, Gory Talons and Fangs, Snapping Maw and Sword-like Claws.

SPECIAL RULES

Mystic Shield: Instead of making a Spell attack, this model can cast Mystic Shield on itself. If it does so, add 1 to this model's Toughness characteristic until the start of its next action.

MANOEUVRE TABLE				
Manoeuvre	**Velocity**			**Execution**
	2	3	4	
Level Flight	Always Safe			Move Move
Swerve	2+	3+	4+	Move Sideslip Move
Bank	3+	4+	5+	Move Move Turn
Turn	4+	5+	6+	Move Turn Move
Snap Turn	5+	6+	7+	Turn Move Move
Stoop	5+	6+	7+	Move Turn OR Turn Move
Circle Back	6+	7+	8+	Turn Move Turn

Pestilential Breath: When this model attacks a ground target, the controlling player can roll 3D6 instead of 2D6 and pick which 2 dice to use for the ground attack roll.

ROYAL TERRORGHEIST

VELOCITY 4
WOUNDS 5
RECOVERY 9+
TOUGHNESS 4

Nightmarish beings born of the oldest Shyishan sorceries, Terrorgheists soar through the skies, seeking out great foes to slay to sate their vampiric thirst. Their piercing cry scythes through the enemy as they swoop into the fray, turning blood to ice.

WEAPON	Arc	Range	Hit Rolls	Damage	Strafe
Death Shriek	Forward 90°	8"	4+	D3	+2
Skeletal Claws	Forward 90°	3"	5+ 5+ 5+	D3	+1
Fanged Maw	Forward 180°	3"	5+ 5+ 5+	D6	+2

WEAPONS

Death Shriek, Skeletal Claws and Fanged Maw.

SPECIAL RULES

Cumbersome: Subtract 2 from acceleration and braking rolls for this model.

Infested: When this model is slain, roll a dice for each enemy flying monster within 3" of this model. On a 4+, that enemy flying monster suffers 1 wound.

MANOEUVRE TABLE				
Manoeuvre	**Velocity**			**Execution**
	2	3	4	
Level Flight	Always Safe			Move Move
Swerve	2+	3+	4+	Move Sideslip Move
Bank	2+	3+	4+	Move Move Turn
Turn	3+	4+	5+	Move Turn Move
Stoop	3+	4+	5+	Move Turn OR Turn Move

ABHORRANT GHOUL KING
ON ROYAL TERRORGHEIST

A spine-chilling shadow against the sky, the Abhorrant Ghoul King and his Terrorgheist embody the eternal darkness of undeath. From the gaping maw of the bat-beast, a shrill scream cuts through the air, shattering the minds of nearby prey.

WEAPON	Arc	Range	Hit Rolls	Damage	Strafe
Arcane Bolt Spell	Forward 180°	12"	4+	D3	+1
Gory Talons and Fangs	360°	3"	5+ 5+ 5+ 5+ 5+	1	+1
Death Shriek	Forward 90°	8"	4+	D3	+2
Skeletal Claws	Forward 90°	3"	5+ 5+ 5+	D3	+1
Fanged Maw	Forward 180°	3"	5+ 5+ 5+	D6	+2

WEAPONS

Arcane Bolt Spell, Gory Talons and Fangs, Death Shriek, Skeletal Claws and Fanged Maw.

SPECIAL RULES

Mystic Shield: Instead of making a Spell attack, this model can cast Mystic Shield on itself. If it does so, add 1 to this model's Toughness characteristic until the start of its next action.

MANOEUVRE TABLE				
Manoeuvre	**Velocity**			**Execution**
	2	3	4	
Level Flight	Always Safe			Move Move
Swerve	3+	4+	5+	Move Sideslip Move
Bank	3+	4+	5+	Move Move Turn
Turn	4+	5+	6+	Move Turn Move
Stoop	4+	5+	6+	Move Turn OR Turn Move

Cumbersome: Subtract 2 from acceleration and braking rolls for this model.

Infested: When this model is slain, roll a dice for each enemy flying monster within 3" of this model. On a 4+, that enemy flying monster suffers 1 wound.

VAMPIRE LORD
ON ZOMBIE DRAGON

Many Vampire Lords see undead dragons as the only mounts worthy to bear them into battle. Those foes not slain by the Vampire are either crushed and torn apart by its steed or withered to nothing by the creature's pestilential breath.

WEAPON	Arc	Range	Hit Rolls	Damage	Strafe
Blood Boil Spell	Forward 180°	12"	6+ 6+ 6+	D3	+1
Vampiric Sword	Forward 180°	3"	4+ 4+ 4+ 4+	D3	+1
Deathlance	Forward 90°	3"	3+ 3+ 3+	D3	+2
Snapping Maw	Forward 180°	3"	5+ 5+ 5+	D6	+2
Sword-like Claws	Forward 90°	3"	5+ 5+ 5+ 5+ 5+	2	+2

WEAPONS

Blood Boil Spell, Vampiric Sword, Snapping Maw and Sword-like Claws. The Vampiric Sword can be replaced with a *Deathlance*.

SPECIAL RULES

Mystic Shield: Instead of making a Spell attack, this model can cast Mystic Shield on itself. If it does so, add 1 to this model's Toughness characteristic until the start of its next action.

MANOEUVRE TABLE				
Manoeuvre	**Velocity**			**Execution**
	2	3	4	
Level Flight	Always Safe			Move Move
Swerve	2+	3+	4+	Move Sideslip Move
Bank	3+	4+	5+	Move Move Turn
Turn	4+	5+	6+	Move Turn Move
Stoop	5+	6+	7+	Move Turn OR Turn Move
Circle Back	6+	7+	8+	Turn Move Turn

Pestilential Breath: When this model attacks a ground target, the controlling player can roll 3D6 instead of 2D6 and pick which 2 dice to use for the ground attack roll.

MEGABOSS
ON MAW-KRUSHA

	VELOCITY **3**	
TOUGHNESS **5**	X	WOUNDS **6**
	RECOVERY **9+**	

A Maw-krusha is a terrifying force of destruction, capable of pulverising almost any foe single-handedly. The Megabosses that ride these beasts are amongst the most deadly of their kind, laying about their foes with deadly choppas and hackas.

WEAPON	Arc	Range	Hit Rolls	Damage	Strafe
Innard-bursting Bellow	Forward 180°	7"	3+ 3+ 3+	1	+2
Boss Gore-hacka and Choppa	360°	3"	3+ 3+ 3+	D6	+1
Boss Choppa and Rip-toof Fist	360°	3"	3+ 3+ 3+ 3+	3	+1
Mighty Fists and Tail	Forward 180°	3"	3+ 3+ 3+ 3+	2	+2

WEAPONS

Innard-bursting Bellow, Boss Gore-hacka and Choppa, and Mighty Fists and Tail.
The Boss Gore-hacka and Choppa can be replaced with a *Boss Choppa and Rip-toof Fist.*

MANOEUVRE TABLE			
Manoeuvre	**Velocity**		**Execution**
	2	**3**	
Level Flight	Always Safe		Move Move
Swerve	2+	3+	Move Sideslip Move
Bank	2+	3+	Move Move Turn
Turn	4+	5+	Move Turn Move
Circle Back	6+	7+	Turn Move Turn

SPECIAL RULES

Destructive Bulk: After this model completes a Level Flight or Swerve manoeuvre, the controlling player can pick 1 enemy flying monster within 3" of this model and roll a dice. On a 4+, that enemy flying monster suffers 1 wound.

OPEN WAR COALITION BATTLE GENERATOR

The Open War coalition battle generator tables are designed to allow 3 or more players to fight an exciting multi-player battle. To use them, players will need to split into two teams called 'coalitions'. Players in the same coalition will need to work together to win the battle, but each will have their own personal goals and agendas.

You can use these battle generator tables instead of those found in the *Warhammer Age of Sigmar Core Book* or the Open War card deck.

COALITION OF DEATH
Before using the battle generator tables, the players must split into two teams, called **coalitions**, following the Coalition of Death rules on page 52. Each player will need to bring along an army with a force points total of about 20 (pg 122).

THE GENERATOR TABLES
Instead of picking a battleplan for the game, use the generator tables as described next. Before doing so, set up terrain using the method of your choice from those described on pages 126-127. We recommend using a battlefield that is 48-60" by 72-96".

Next, roll on the generator tables. The coalition battle generator is made up of 5 tables: the Map table determines how the armies are set up, the Objective and Personal Agenda tables determine what the players must do in order to win the battle, and the Ruse and Twist tables determine whether any special rules apply to the battle. It also uses the Open War army generator (pg 122-125) and the Open War terrain methods (pg 126-127).

MAP
One warlord rolls a dice to determine which Map table will be used: on an even roll, the map will be generated from Map Table 1 (left, opposite); on an odd roll, the map will be generated from Map Table 2 (right, opposite). The opposing warlord then rolls a dice and looks up the result on the appropriate Map table. This will be the map for this battle.

OBJECTIVE
One warlord rolls a dice and looks up the result on the Objective table (pg 42). This will be the objective for this battle. Sometimes the Objective table will require the warlord to set up 1 or more objectives on the battlefield. If both warlords are required to set up objectives, they must roll off. Starting with the warlord who won the roll-off, the warlords alternate setting up the objectives.

TWIST
One warlord rolls a dice and looks up the result on the Twist table (pg 42). The resulting special rule will apply for the duration of the battle.

PERSONAL AGENDA
Each player rolls a dice and looks up the result on the Personal Agenda table (pg 43). If the player's coalition wins the battle, they win a **major victory** if they have completed their personal agenda and a **minor victory** if they have not. If the player's coalition loses the battle, they suffer a **minor loss** if they have completed their personal agenda and a **major loss** if they have not.

SET-UP
The warlords roll off and the winner decides which territory each coalition will use. The warlords then roll off again. Each player in the winning coalition rolls 3 times on the army generator (pg 122-125) and sets up the units generated wholly within their coalition's territory, more than 9" from enemy territory. The opposing coalition does the same, after which set-up is complete.

RUSE
If, after set-up, one coalition has more force points' worth of units than the other, the warlord of the coalition with the lower total rolls on the Ruse table (pg 43). That ruse can be used by that warlord or the warlord can allow a player from their coalition to use it instead.

FIRST TURN
The warlords roll off and the winner decides which coalition will have the first turn in the first battle round.

REINFORCEMENTS
At the end of each of their turns, each player in a coalition can generate reinforcements by rolling on the army generator (pg 122-125) and setting up the units generated wholly within their coalition's territory, wholly within 6" of the arrival edge shown for their coalition on the map being used, and more than 3" from any enemy units.

Players can generate reinforcements in this way as long as the force points total for their army is less than 20 (pg 122). If a roll causes their army's force points total to equal or exceed 20, the player should set up the units from that roll but should not generate any further reinforcements for the rest of the battle.

GLORIOUS VICTORY
In order to win the battle, a coalition must achieve the victory condition rolled on the Objective table. If the battle ends before this happens, the battle is a draw.

Once the result of the battle has been determined, each player calculates whether they have won a **major victory** or **minor victory** or suffered a **major loss** or **minor loss**, as described in the Personal Agenda section above.

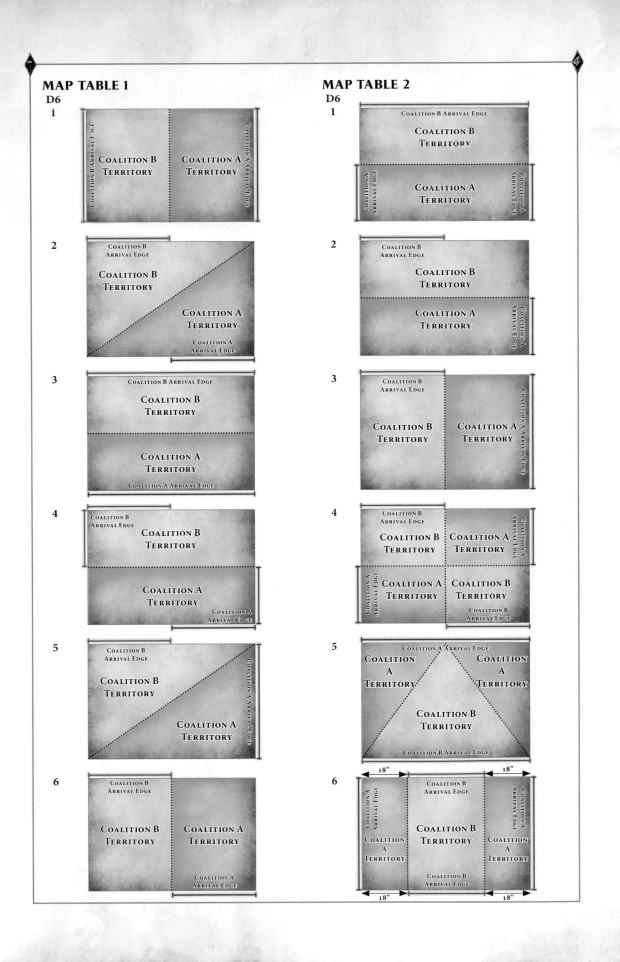

MAP TABLE 1

D6

1 — Coalition B Territory | Coalition A Territory (Coalition B Arrival Edge / Coalition A Arrival Edge)

2 — Coalition B Territory (Coalition B Arrival Edge) / Coalition A Territory (Coalition A Arrival Edge)

3 — Coalition B Territory (Coalition B Arrival Edge) / Coalition A Territory (Coalition A Arrival Edge)

4 — Coalition B Territory (Coalition B Arrival Edge) / Coalition A Territory (Coalition A Arrival Edge)

5 — Coalition B Territory (Coalition B Arrival Edge) / Coalition A Territory (Coalition A Arrival Edge)

6 — Coalition B Territory (Coalition B Arrival Edge) / Coalition A Territory (Coalition A Arrival Edge)

MAP TABLE 2

D6

1 — Coalition B Territory (Coalition B Arrival Edge) / Coalition A Territory (Coalition A Arrival Edge)

2 — Coalition B Territory (Coalition B Arrival Edge) / Coalition A Territory (Coalition A Arrival Edge)

3 — Coalition B Territory (Coalition B Arrival Edge) / Coalition A Territory (Coalition A Arrival Edge)

4 — Coalition B Territory (Coalition B Arrival Edge) | Coalition A Territory (Coalition A Arrival Edge) / Coalition A Territory (Coalition A Arrival Edge) | Coalition B Territory (Coalition B Arrival Edge)

5 — Coalition A Territory / Coalition A Territory (Coalition A Arrival Edge) / Coalition B Territory (Coalition B Arrival Edge)

6 — 18" | 18" — Coalition A Arrival Edge / Coalition B Arrival Edge / Coalition A Territory | Coalition B Territory | Coalition A Territory (Coalition A Arrival Edge) / Coalition B Arrival Edge — 18" | 18"

OBJECTIVE TABLE

D6   Objective

1 **Blood and Land:** Divide the battlefield into 4 equal-sized quarters and place 1 objective in the centre of each quarter. At the end of the fifth battle round, each coalition scores 1 victory point for each objective that they control and 1 victory point for each enemy general or enemy HERO that has been slain. The coalition with the most victory points wins the battle.

2 **Field of Glory:** Place 1 objective in the centre of the battlefield, then the warlords roll off. Starting with the winner, each warlord places 1 objective wholly within their territory, more than 6" from any battlefield edge. At the end of the fifth battle round, the coalition that controls the most objectives wins the battle.

3 **Occupation:** The warlords roll off. Starting with the winner, they take it in turns to place 1 objective on the battlefield, more than 12" from any other objectives, until there are 3 objectives on the battlefield. Objectives must be placed within 1" of a terrain feature if it is possible to do so. At the end of the fifth battle round, the coalition that controls the most objectives wins the battle.

4 **Drawn and Quartered:** The warlords roll off. Starting with the winner, they take it in turns to place 1 objective on the battlefield, more than 6" from the centre of the battlefield, more

than 6" from any battlefield edge and more than 18" from any other objectives, until there are 4 objectives on the battlefield. At the end of each of their turns, each coalition scores 1 victory point for each objective that they control. The coalition with the most victory points at the end of the fifth battle round wins the battle.

5 **Final Objective:** The warlords roll off. Starting with the winner, they take it in turns to place 1 objective on the battlefield, more than 6" from the centre of the battlefield, more than 6" from any battlefield edge and more than 9" from any other objectives, until there are 6 objectives on the battlefield. At the start of each battle round, after determining which coalition has the first turn, the warlord whose coalition will take the first turn must remove 1 objective from the battlefield. At the end of the fifth battle round, the coalition that controls the final remaining objective wins the battle.

6 **Destroyers:** The warlords roll off. Starting with the winner, they take it in turns to place 1 objective on the battlefield, more than 6" from the centre of the battlefield, more than 6" from any battlefield edge and more than 6" from any other objectives, until there are 10 objectives on the battlefield. At the start of their hero phase, each warlord can raze 1 objective controlled by their coalition that is not wholly within their own territory and remove it from play. At the end of the fifth battle round, the coalition that razed the most objectives wins the battle.

TWIST TABLE

D6   Twist

1 **Double Twist:** The warlords roll off. Starting with the winner, each warlord must pick a different twist from this table.

2 **Arcane Predator:** The warlords roll off. The winner must set up a predatory endless spell in the centre of the battlefield. The endless spell cannot be dispelled and must remain wholly within 18" of the centre of the battlefield.

3 **Uneasy Alliances:** Subtract 2 from charge rolls and add 2 to battleshock rolls for units that are within 6" of any units that are from the same coalition but are not part of the same army.

4 **Forced March:** Units that are set up on the battlefield after the battle begins can be set up wholly within 9" of their arrival edge instead of wholly within 6" (they must still be set up within their coalition's territory and more than 3" from any enemy units).

5 **Healing Winds:** At the start of each of their hero phases, each player can pick a model from their army. Heal up to D3 wounds allocated to that model.

6 **Traitors:** At the end of the first battle round, randomly select 1 player from each coalition. Those players switch coalitions.

PERSONAL AGENDA TABLE

D6	Personal Agenda Victory Condition
1	**Defend:** You complete your personal agenda if there are no enemy units wholly within your coalition's territory at the end of the third or fourth battle round.
2	**Slay Their Leaders:** You complete your personal agenda if all enemy **HEROES** are slain.
3	**Protect the Messenger:** At the start of the first battle round, before determining who has the first turn, pick 1 model from your army that is on the battlefield to be the messenger. The model cannot be your army's general. You complete your personal agenda if your messenger is still on the battlefield at the end of the fourth battle round.
4	**Blunt:** You complete your personal agenda if all of the enemy units that were set up on the battlefield at the start of the battle are destroyed.
5	**Destined for Greatness:** You complete your personal agenda if your general is still on the battlefield at the end of the third battle round.
6	**Invasion:** You complete your personal agenda if all units from your army that have not been destroyed are wholly within enemy territory at the end of the third battle round.

RUSE TABLE

D6	Ruse
1	**Inspired Leadership:** If this warlord's general is on the battlefield, each player in their coalition receives 1 extra command point at the start of each of their hero phases.
2	**Catch Them Off Guard:** This warlord can use this ruse after set-up is complete but before the battle begins. They must pick a player from their coalition. That player can move any of their units up to D6" (roll separately for each unit).
3	**Quartermaster General:** If this warlord has any units on the battlefield, each player in their coalition can re-roll their rolls on the army generator.
4	**Priority Target:** After set-up is complete but before the battle begins, this warlord can pick 1 enemy **HERO** that is on the battlefield from each enemy army. The Look Out, Sir! rule does not apply to those **HEROES**.
5	**Unyielding:** While this warlord has any units on the battlefield. add 1 to the Bravery characteristic of all units in their coalition.
6	**Bribery:** Once per battle, at the start of the combat phase, this warlord can pick 1 player in the opposing coalition. Subtract 1 from hit rolls for units from that player's army until the end of that phase.

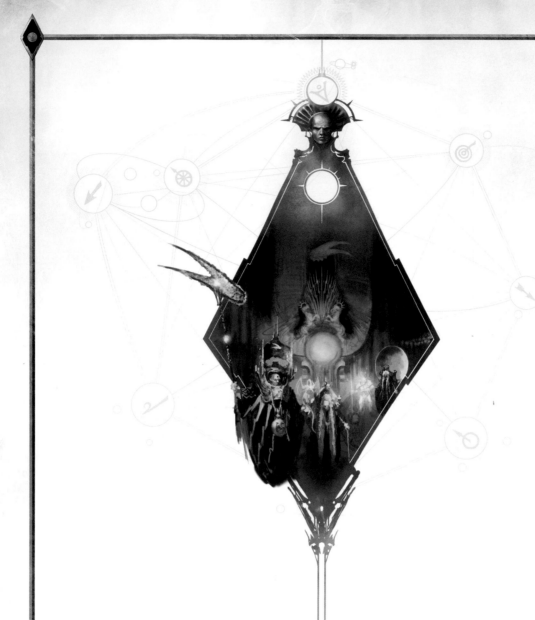

NARRATIVE PLAY GAMES

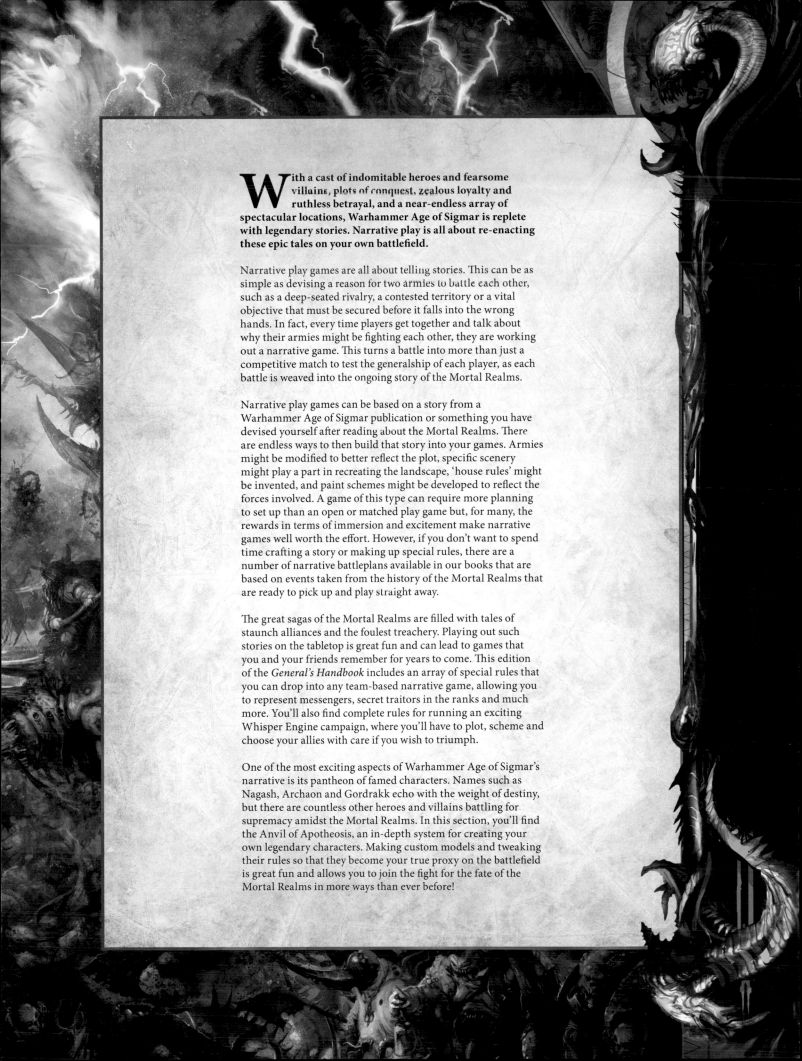

With a cast of indomitable heroes and fearsome villains, plots of conquest, zealous loyalty and ruthless betrayal, and a near-endless array of spectacular locations, Warhammer Age of Sigmar is replete with legendary stories. Narrative play is all about re-enacting these epic tales on your own battlefield.

Narrative play games are all about telling stories. This can be as simple as devising a reason for two armies to battle each other, such as a deep-seated rivalry, a contested territory or a vital objective that must be secured before it falls into the wrong hands. In fact, every time players get together and talk about why their armies might be fighting each other, they are working out a narrative game. This turns a battle into more than just a competitive match to test the generalship of each player, as each battle is weaved into the ongoing story of the Mortal Realms.

Narrative play games can be based on a story from a Warhammer Age of Sigmar publication or something you have devised yourself after reading about the Mortal Realms. There are endless ways to then build that story into your games. Armies might be modified to better reflect the plot, specific scenery might play a part in recreating the landscape, 'house rules' might be invented, and paint schemes might be developed to reflect the forces involved. A game of this type can require more planning to set up than an open or matched play game but, for many, the rewards in terms of immersion and excitement make narrative games well worth the effort. However, if you don't want to spend time crafting a story or making up special rules, there are a number of narrative battleplans available in our books that are based on events taken from the history of the Mortal Realms that are ready to pick up and play straight away.

The great sagas of the Mortal Realms are filled with tales of staunch alliances and the foulest treachery. Playing out such stories on the tabletop is great fun and can lead to games that you and your friends remember for years to come. This edition of the *General's Handbook* includes an array of special rules that you can drop into any team-based narrative game, allowing you to represent messengers, secret traitors in the ranks and much more. You'll also find complete rules for running an exciting Whisper Engine campaign, where you'll have to plot, scheme and choose your allies with care if you wish to triumph.

One of the most exciting aspects of Warhammer Age of Sigmar's narrative is its pantheon of famed characters. Names such as Nagash, Archaon and Gordrakk echo with the weight of destiny, but there are countless other heroes and villains battling for supremacy amidst the Mortal Realms. In this section, you'll find the Anvil of Apotheosis, an in-depth system for creating your own legendary characters. Making custom models and tweaking their rules so that they become your true proxy on the battlefield is great fun and allows you to join the fight for the fate of the Mortal Realms in more ways than ever before!

TEAM BATTLES SPECIAL RULES

Throughout the history of the Mortal Realms, disparate armies have come together to fight against a common foe. Whether these are age-old allies bound by pacts of blood or ragged coalitions forged from dire convenience, each battle they fight is decided as much by their ability to work together as it is by strategy and skill.

This section introduces several new rules that will help you fight narrative games involving teams of players. Across the Mortal Realms, there have been countless battles fought between coalitions of armies, each made up of uneasy allegiances and fraught with tension. These rules will recreate those battles for you and your gaming group, adding in rules to represent the difficult lines of communication and the forging and breaking of alliances in the heat of battle. The rules are designed to be used as part of a Whisper Engine campaign (pg 48-51) and to work with the Coalition of Death battleplans found in this book and the *Warhammer Age of Sigmar Core Book*. They can also be used in any team battle.

The rules in this section are divided into three parts: the Fog of War rules, the Alliance and Betrayal rules and the Games Master rules. The Fog of War rules and the Alliance and Betrayal rules are modular, meaning you can use one without using the other. The Games Master rules work in tandem with the other two sections, bringing the narrative alive in your team battles.

FOG OF WAR RULES

Lines of Communication: *In the cloying fog of war, coordination can swiftly break down between even the most trusted of allies.*

Before the battle begins, players are given 10 minutes in which they can freely discuss strategy and tactics. Once the battle begins, players in a coalition can only discuss strategy and tactics if the generals of each of their armies are within 3" of each other. Otherwise, players must use handwritten letters to communicate.

At the start of each hero phase, players are given 5 minutes to write any letters. The warlords of each coalition then roll off. Starting with the loser, the warlords take it in turns to pick 1 player in their coalition to send their letters, until all players have sent their letters. The player must declare which of their letters are to be sent by land and which are to be sent by air.

For each letter sent by **land**, the player hands the message to the recipient, who cannot open the letter until the end of the movement phase of that turn.

For each letter sent by **air**, the player rolls a dice. On a 1 or 2, the message has been lost and is immediately destroyed. On a 3+, the player hands the message to the recipient, who can open the letter at the end of that hero phase.

Designer's Note: *If players accidentally talk about tactics, you may want to incur a penalty. For example, each time a player discusses tactics, 1 extra command point could be given to a player in the opposing coalition (chosen by their warlord). If you decide to introduce such a penalty, this should be agreed with all players beforehand and common sense should be applied as to how much discussion warrants awarding a command point.*

Declaring Charges: *In the chaos of battle, it is often impossible to know where an ally intends to direct their strength until their warriors charge forth, screaming their war cries.*

At the start of a coalition's charge phase, all players in that coalition must secretly note down which of their units intend to make a charge move in that phase and which enemy units they intend to charge. The players then reveal this information simultaneously. In that charge phase, when a unit makes a charge move, it must finish that charge move within ½" of the enemy unit it intended to charge, otherwise the charge fails.

ALLIANCE AND BETRAYAL RULES

Uneasy Alliances: *Desperate times call for desperate alliances, but these fractious armies are inevitably harder to lead than an average force.*

At the start of the battle, after armies have been set up but before the first battle round begins, each warlord counts the number of Grand Alliances present in their coalition. If there are 2 or more, each player in that coalition must roll a dice. On a 1-3, that player does not gain 1 command point in their first hero phase.

Betrayal: *The sudden shock of betrayal is a powerful weapon in war, but those who would desert their allies without due consideration may soon find themselves friendless and vulnerable in turn.*

At the start of a battle round, before any predatory endless spells are moved, a player who is not a warlord can declare that they are defecting from their coalition. To do so, their general must be on the battlefield and they must spend 3 command points. Once the player has defected, the warlord of the opposing coalition must decide if they will welcome the defecting player or forsake them. Before they make their decision, they are allowed 5 minutes to discuss this with the other players in the coalition (this discussion is exempt from the Lines of Communication special rule, if in play). Once the warlord has made their decision, one of the following scenarios will occur:

Welcomed: If the coalition welcomes the defecting player, that player joins that coalition. However, until the end of the battle, add 1 to hit and wound rolls for attacks made with melee weapons that target units in the defecting player's army.

Forsaken: If the coalition forsakes the defecting player, that player remains in their existing coalition. However, they are considered to have suffered a **major loss** regardless of their coalition's victory status. In addition, until the end of the battle, the Bravery characteristic of all units in the defecting player's army are reduced to 0.

Bought Favours: *A bribe here or underhanded favour there can be costly in the short term, but in the long run, it can win commanders a powerful, unexpected ally.*

At the start of any phase, a player may declare that they are giving 1 or more of their unspent command points to another player in their coalition.

GAMES MASTER RULES
The **games master** (abbreviated to **GM**) is a neutral player who does not control an army and who acts as an adjudicator in the following rules.

Hidden Command Points: *As stratagems are revealed, the balance of power can shift without warning.*

The GM keeps a tally of every player's command points. This allows the players to spend their command points secretly.

Assassination Attempt: *Though not without risk, a knife in the back can be worth a thousand swords in the front.*

At the start of each hero phase, players can write a letter to the GM declaring that they will make an assassination attempt. To do so,

they must state who they are and which general is the target of the assassination. In addition, they must spend 3 command points.

At the end of that hero phase, the GM reveals that an assassination attempt is taking place and tells the players which general is the target (but not which player is making the assassination attempt).

The GM then rolls 2D6 and adds the number of wounds currently allocated to the target to the roll. If the result is equal to or greater than the Wounds characteristic of the target, it is immediately slain. Otherwise, the attempt has failed. If the attempt fails, the GM must roll on the table below to determine the outcome.

ASSASSINATION TABLE

D6	Result
1-2	The GM reveals which player made the assassination attempt.
3-4	The GM only reveals which coalition the player who made the assassination attempt is in.
5-6	No effect.

Bought Favours: The Bought Favour special rule is changed as follows with the inclusion of a GM:

At the start of each hero phase, players can write a letter to the GM declaring that they are giving 1 or more of their unspent command points to another player. To do so, they must state who they are, to whom they will give their unspent command points and how many of their unspent command points they will give. Players can give command points to players on the other coalition if they wish. Once the GM has made a note of the exchange, the letter is handed to the recipient of the command points to notify them.

Lines of Communication: The Lines of Communication special rule is amended as follows with the inclusion of a GM:

Letters sent by land are handed to the GM, who must collect all letters before handing them to the recipients. This allows players to send letters to players on the other coalition, unbeknownst to their teammates.

The GM opens and reads each letter handed to them. The GM must secretly roll a dice for each letter not addressed to the GM. On a 1, the GM must then secretly roll on the table below to determine what happens to that letter.

LETTER TABLE

D6	Result
1	**Intercepted!:** The letter is given to the warlord of the opposing coalition instead of the recipient.
2-3	**Lost:** The letter is discarded.
4-6	**Delayed:** The letter is not delivered until the start of the next battle round.

THE WHISPER ENGINE

Created by the cursed Chamonic genius Renius Lazarra, the Whisper Engine was an artefact with the power to sort truth from lies – until it was corrupted by the servants of Tzeentch and became a tool of duplicity and deception. Now it is lost in the transmutative wilds of the Realm of Metal, working its sinister magic on those armies that march to reclaim it.

A Whisper Engine campaign has 4-7 players and revolves around playing large team games in which every player is involved. Before each battle, players can spend resources to shape which players are on which team, and in the aftermath of each battle, players can further their own goals on the campaign map. The cunning general will ensure they are surrounded by powerful allies before crushing their enemies both on the battlefield and on the campaign map. You can expect negotiation and skullduggery galore as players forge makeshift alliances and backstab each other in an attempt to seize victory for themselves.

ORGANISING A CAMPAIGN

When organising a campaign, the first thing you need to do is find some other players to take part. A Whisper Engine campaign is designed to have between 4 and 7 players. If you have an odd number of players, you need not worry – the unique bidding system used in this campaign caters for odd and even numbers of players.

Next, you will need to decide how long you want the campaign to last. We have found it is better to choose to fight a short campaign of 6-8 weeks, with each campaign round lasting 1 week. This will keep all the players excited – and besides, there is nothing stopping you from starting a new campaign immediately after the first has been completed!

THE CAMPAIGN MAP

A Whisper Engine campaign uses a campaign map (pg 51) composed of territories and key locations that players will seek to conquer and control. We recommend you make a photocopy of the campaign map. The campaign map is made up of 19 territories, 7 of which are referred to as special locations. If a player controls a territory (see opposite) that is also a special location, they gain a bonus from it.

Each special location is identified by its unique icon. Consult the table below to see the bonuses that the different special locations give.

SPECIAL LOCATIONS TABLE	
Special Location	Bonus
	The Foundry Alembic: *Within these sigil-marked walls, the power of magic is harnessed with greater ease.* The player who controls this territory can add 1 to casting rolls for friendly **WIZARDS**.
	The Fluxspire: *The dark experiments once performed within this tower grant its owner knowledge of the future.* The player who controls this territory receives 1 extra command point at the start of the battle.
	Cairns of the Argent Priests: *Divine power still resides within this network of gilded barrows and necropolises.* The player who controls this territory can add 1 to prayer rolls for friendly **PRIESTS**.
	The Lost Workshop of Lazarra: *The workshop of Renius Lazarra has long lain abandoned, but secrets still reside within for those who can claim it.* The player who controls this territory receives 1 additional glory point when totalling glory points at the end of a campaign round.
	The Cogwork Unmaking: *Treasures from a lost age can be found in the wreckage of this automaton army.* The player who controls this territory can give 1 additional artefact of power to 1 **HERO** in their army.
	The Gate of Silvered Dreams: *The argent portal of this Realmgate can be used to bring forth reinforcing armies.* The player who controls this territory receives 1 additional force point at the start of the bidding step.
	The Gilded Cage: *Malign entities prowl the depths of this shattered vault, waiting to be unleashed once more.* The player who controls this territory can include 1 endless spell in their army for the force points cost, or Pitched Battle points cost, of 0.

SETTING UP THE CAMPAIGN MAP

After organising the campaign, you need to gather the players together and set up the campaign map. Each player starts the campaign with a number of territories under their control. Consult the table below to see how many territories each player starts with.

TERRITORIES TABLE	
Number of Players	Starting Territories
4-5	3
6-7	2

The players sort themselves into a sequential order using a series of roll-offs. Then, starting with the first player in the order and working through to the last player in the order, each player picks 1 territory on the map and marks it to show it is under their control. Players cannot pick a territory that has already been picked by another player.

Keep repeating this step until all players have picked the relevant number of territories to be under their control.

PLAYING THE CAMPAIGN

A Whisper Engine campaign is divided into campaign rounds, each of which consists of the 3 following steps:

1. The Bidding Step
2. The Battle Step
3. The Aftermath Step

THE BIDDING STEP

In this step, the players determine which of the two coalitions each player will be part of in that campaign round. Resolve the bidding step as follows.

Firstly, the players gather around a table upon which there are 2 tokens, one to represent Coalition A in the upcoming battle and one to represent Coalition B.

Each player uses a counter or miniature to represent their army. Each player also starts this step with 20 force points, which can be used to make bids to alter the coalitions.

The players then sort themselves into a bidding order using a series of roll-offs. Now bidding can begin.

Bidding is carried out in a series of rounds. In each round, 2 players will be placed, one in each coalition. To start the first bidding round, the player who is first in the bidding order picks any 2 players and assigns 1 player to Coalition A and 1 player to Coalition B.

Then, continuing with the next player in the bidding order, each player either bids or passes. If a player bids, they can spend a number of force points (see below) to replace 1 of the assigned players with another player, to replace both of the assigned players with 2 other players or to swap the assigned players with each other. Regardless of any alterations made, at the end of the bid, 1 player must still be assigned to Coalition A and 1 player to Coalition B.

The first time a player bids in a bidding round, it costs 1 force point. The second time a player bids in that bidding round, it costs 2 force points, and so on.

If a player passes, the next player in the bidding order then chooses to bid or pass. The bidding order is circular: after the last player in the bidding order has chosen to bid or pass, it moves back round to the first player in the bidding order. Keep moving around the group in bidding order until every player consecutively passes. At this point, the bidding round ends. When the bidding round ends, the player assigned to Coalition A and the player assigned to Coalition B are **locked**.

A new bidding round then begins, this time starting with the next player in the bidding order. The number of force points needed for a player to make their first bid is reset back to 1, but from now on, each time a player makes a bid, they cannot replace or swap any locked players.

Keep resolving bidding rounds until all players have been assigned to a coalition. If your campaign has an odd number of players, the last bidding round is slightly different: players will simply bid to assign the odd player to either Coalition A or Coalition B. Once all bidding rounds have been completed, each player will be assigned to Coalition A or Coalition B for the upcoming battle.

THE BATTLE STEP

The battles fought in a Whisper Engine campaign use the Coalition of Death rules as found on page 52. In addition, the Fog of War rules and the Alliance and Betrayal rules from pages 46-47 are used.

In each battle step, a single Coalition of Death battle is fought between the two coalitions as determined in the previous bidding step. The players that were first locked to Coalition A and Coalition B are the **warlords** of their respective coalitions.

The warlords roll off and the winner chooses the battleplan that will be used for the battle. Players can then begin mustering their armies.

Each player uses the Open War army generator (pg 122-125) to muster their army. The number of force points that the player has remaining after the bidding step is the force size limit of their army.

Alternatively, if the players are using Pitched Battle profiles for this campaign, they can instead muster an army equal to 100 times their remaining force points. For example, if a player has 12 force points remaining, they could muster an army of up to 1,200 Pitched Battle points for that battle.

THE AFTERMATH STEP

After the battle has ended, players should gather around the campaign map to complete the aftermath step.

First, all the players who won a **major victory** or **minor victory** in that battle sort themselves into a sequential order using a series of roll-offs. Starting with the first player in the order, each player picks 1 territory on the map to be under their control. The territory picked either must not already be under anyone's control or must be under the control of a player who did not win a **major victory** or **minor victory** in the last battle. In addition, the territory that player picks must be adjacent to a territory already under their control. If there are no eligible territories, that player must forego this step.

Next, the players who did not win a **major victory** or **minor victory** do the same. This time, players cannot pick a territory under the control of another player. This means that if a player loses their last territory before it is their turn to pick, they will be unable to pick a territory to be under their control. In this case, that player is said to be **routed**.

ROUTED

At the end of the aftermath step, if a player does not have any territories under their control, they are said to be **routed**. Any routed players must sort themselves into a sequential order using a series of roll-offs and then take it in turns to pick 1 territory to be under their control. If there are any territories not already under anyone's control, these must be picked first. Otherwise, any territory can be picked as long as it is not controlled by another player who only has 1 territory under their control.

TOTAL GLORY POINTS

At the end of the aftermath step, each player must add up the glory points they earned in that campaign round. Keep a running tally of each player's glory points from campaign round to campaign round.

Players earn glory points as follows:

Dominated Territory: Each player earns 1 glory point for each area of territory that is under their control.

Consolidation of Power: Each player counts the single largest group of adjacent territories under their control and earns a number of glory points equivalent to the number of territories in that group. For example, if a player has a group of 3 territories under their control on one side of the campaign map and a group of 4 territories on the other side of the campaign map, they would earn 4 glory points.

DECLARING THE WINNER

Once all the campaign rounds have been completed, the glory points earned by each player are tallied up and the winning player is announced. To give the campaign a memorable send-off, all players should be brought together when the winner is announced. You could even schedule the last battle step and aftermath step to happen immediately before the campaign is concluded to allow for some tense and nail-biting final moments.

Finishing a campaign is a momentous achievement and it shouldn't only be the winner of the campaign who is celebrated. For example, you could include bonus awards for the 'coolest army', the 'best-painted **Hero**' or the 'most sporting opponent', all voted for by the players.

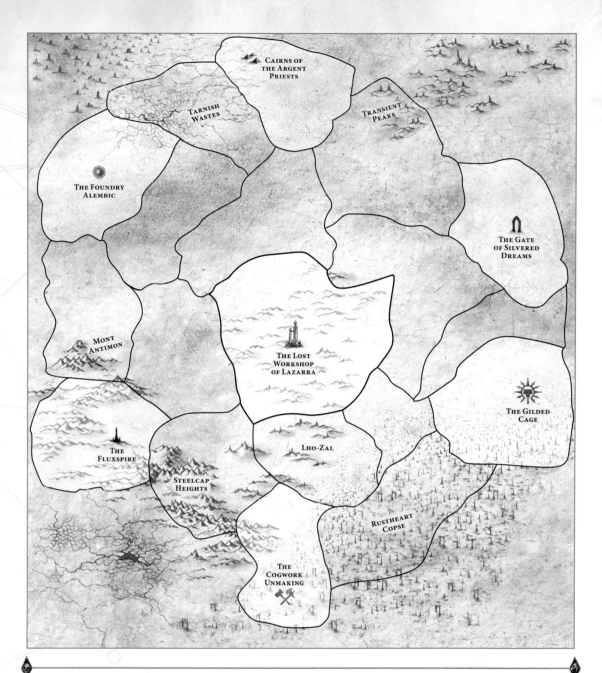

The map shows the following labeled regions:

- CAIRNS OF THE ARGENT PRIESTS
- TARNISH WASTES
- TRANSIENT PEAKS
- THE FOUNDRY ALEMBIC
- THE GATE OF SILVERED DREAMS
- MONT ANTIMON
- THE LOST WORKSHOP OF LAZARRA
- THE GILDED CAGE
- THE FLUXSPIRE
- LHO-ZAL
- STEELCAP HEIGHTS
- RUSTHEART COPSE
- THE COGWORK UNMAKING

*L*ike much of Chamon, the desolate valleys of Argetoria have fallen under the influence of the Changer of the Ways. But while some regions of the Realm of Metal have been mutated beyond recognition or set ablaze by gouts of multi-hued witchfire, the curse that has settled on this land is more subtle in nature – a product of the Whisper Engine that lies hidden amidst the wastes. Rolling banks of silver mist drift across Argetoria, shrouding its valleys and rust-barked forests in a chemical haze. Those who wander in these mists for too long soon find their minds aflame with thoughts of ambition and primacy; even the most trusted allies will eventually turn on one another under the malign influence of Renius Lazarra's cursed device. Indeed, some have even claimed that the Whisper Engine has become sentient over years of daemonic influence, that it delights in leading armies to the ancient ruins and shattered temples that lie scattered throughout Argetoria, only to see these competing forces battle amongst themselves. Many such crusading forces seek the Whisper Engine itself, either to end its menace or claim its power for their own. Yet somehow the device always seems to elude them, and more than one commander has gone mad eternally wandering the wastes with a head full of treacherous thoughts.

COALITION OF DEATH

The Mortal Realms are inhabited by myriad diverse races and factions, each with their own agendas, alliances and enmities. Multiplayer games help tap into this incredible variety and invite exciting, radically different styles of battle to boot.

Warhammer Age of Sigmar games are conventionally played between 2 people, but battling it out with several players lends the game a new and exciting dynamic. This section introduces a few easy modifications to the core rules to allow for battles between 2 sides of players, referred to as **coalitions**.

To play a Coalition of Death game, you must have 3 or more players. The battle can be fought using any of the battleplans for Warhammer Age of Sigmar – all you need to do is split the players into 2 coalitions, with each taking one side in the forthcoming battle. We have included 3 new battleplans on the following pages that are designed for use with these Coalition of Death rules, and a further 3 battleplans can be found in the *Warhammer Age of Sigmar Core Book* (pg 273-275).

THE ARMIES

The players are organised into 2 coalitions, using any method preferred. The coalitions can be made up of different numbers of players. Each player then picks an army as described in the core rules.

Each player commands the models in their army and is allowed to decide what they do, how they move, and so on, and that player makes all of the dice rolls for their own units. In addition, each player accrues their own command points and can use any allegiance abilities available to them as normal.

Models in other players' armies that are part of your coalition are considered to be neither friendly nor enemy models. This means that abilities used by your army that only affect friendly models or that only affect enemy models will not affect models from the other armies in your coalition.

GENERALS AND WARLORDS

Each player picks a general for their army as normal. You must also pick 1 player from each coalition to be the **warlord**. If, at any time during the game, the coalition cannot decide in what order to carry out actions, the warlord has the final say on the order of events. In addition, if a dice needs to be rolled for the whole coalition, the warlord makes that dice roll. Finally, any victory conditions from a battleplan that apply to an army general only apply to the warlord's general, unless specifically noted otherwise.

FIGHTING THE BATTLE

Instead of each player taking a turn during a Coalition of Death game, each coalition takes a turn. At the start of the first battle round, the warlord of the coalition that finished setting up all their armies first chooses which coalition has the first turn. At the start of each battle round after the first, the warlords must roll off, and the winner decides which coalition takes the first turn. If the roll-off is a tie, the warlord of the coalition that went first in the last battle round can choose which coalition goes first in the current battle round.

Where individual players would normally alternate taking actions, the coalitions alternate taking actions, with each player in the coalition being allowed to carry them out. For example, in the combat phase, each player in one coalition can attack with 1 of their units, then each player in the other coalition, and so on.

The same principle applies during set-up. For example, if you are fighting a battle where the players take turns to set up units, then in a Coalition of Death battle, the coalitions take turns to set up, with each player in that coalition setting up 1 unit when it is their coalition's turn to do so. In addition, once all units in one coalition have been set up, the coalitions stop alternating setting up units and the other coalition sets up the rest of its units.

Lastly, rules that refer to the 'opposing player' or 'opponent' are treated as referring to the **opposing coalition** instead. For example, when a WIZARD casts a spell, the opposing coalition can attempt to unbind that spell, following the normal rules for doing so, rather than each player on the opposing coalition making an attempt to unbind that spell.

Ossiarch Bonereapers
Mortisan Soulreaper

BATTLEPLAN
DIVIDE AND CONQUER

Two coalitions meet in battle, each seeking to consolidate their own territory and drive the enemy away in disarray.

COALITION OF DEATH

This is a battle for 3 or more players. Use the Coalition of Death rules from page 52.

OBJECTIVES

Set up 5 objectives as shown on the map.

SET-UP

The warlords roll off, and the winner decides which territory each coalition will use. The territories are shown on the map. The coalition of the warlord who won the roll-off sets up first. The opposing coalition sets up second. Units must be set up wholly within the coalition's own territory and more than 9" from enemy territory.

RESERVES

Should a player wish, any of their units may start the battle in reserve instead of being set up on the battlefield. Starting from the second battle round, reserve units can join the battle during any of their coalition's movement phases. All of the models in the unit must be set up within their coalition's territory, within 3" of the battlefield edge and more than 9" from any enemy units. This counts as their move for that movement phase.

GLORIOUS VICTORY

The coalition with the most victory points at the end of the battle wins a **major victory**. If both coalitions have the same number of victory points, use the tiebreaker to determine which coalition wins a **minor victory** or if the battle is a **draw**.

VICTORY POINTS

Victory points are scored as follows:

- Each time a coalition slays an enemy model that has a Wounds characteristic of 10 or more, that coalition scores 1 victory point.

- If a coalition slays an enemy general, that coalition scores 1 victory point. If that general was the enemy warlord's general, that coalition scores 1 additional victory point.

- At the end of each of their turns, each coalition scores 2 victory points if they control the objective in the centre of the battlefield and 1 victory point for each other objective that they control.

TIEBREAKER

If the coalitions are tied on victory points at the end of the battle, each coalition must add up the points value of any enemy units that were destroyed during the battle (excluding any new units that were added to the armies after the battle started). If one coalition has a higher total, that coalition wins a **minor victory**. If neither coalition has a higher total, the battle is a **draw**.

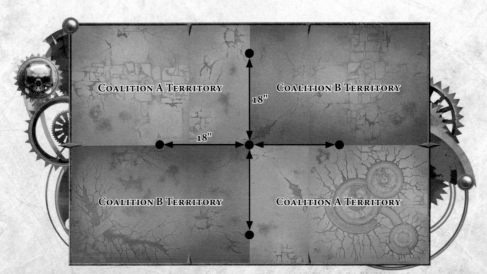

COALITION A TERRITORY

COALITION B TERRITORY

18"

18"

COALITION B TERRITORY

COALITION A TERRITORY

BATTLEPLAN
DIMINISHING GAINS

As a fierce battle rages between two coalitions, each must act quickly before the gains they seek are reduced to naught.

COALITION OF DEATH

This is a battle for 3 or more players. Use the Coalition of Death rules from page 52.

OBJECTIVES

Set up 6 objectives as shown on the map.

At the start of each battle round after the first, the warlord of the coalition taking the second turn in that battle round can pick 1 objective on the battlefield and remove it from play.

SET-UP

The warlords roll off, and the winner decides which territory each coalition will use. The territories are shown on the map. The coalition of the warlord who won the roll-off sets up first. The opposing coalition sets up second. Units must be set up wholly within the coalition's own territory and more than 9" from enemy territory.

RESERVES

Should a player wish, any of their units may start the battle in reserve instead of being set up on the battlefield. Starting from the second battle round, reserve units can join the battle during any of their coalition's movement phases. All of the models in the unit must be set up within their coalition's territory, within 3" of the battlefield edge and more than 9" from any enemy units. This counts as their move for that movement phase.

GLORIOUS VICTORY

The coalition with the most victory points at the end of the battle wins a **major victory**. If both coalitions have the same number of victory points, use the tiebreaker to determine which coalition wins a **minor victory** or if the battle is a **draw**.

VICTORY POINTS

Victory points are scored as follows:

- Each time a coalition slays an enemy model that has a Wounds characteristic of 10 or more, that coalition scores 1 victory point.

- If a coalition slays an enemy general, that coalition scores 1 victory point. If that general was the enemy warlord's general, that coalition scores 1 additional victory point.

- At the end of each of their turns, each coalition scores 1 victory point for each objective that they control.

TIEBREAKER

If the coalitions are tied on victory points at the end of the battle, each coalition must add up the points value of any enemy units that were destroyed during the battle (excluding any new units that were added to the armies after the battle started). If one coalition has a higher total, that coalition wins a **minor victory**. If neither coalition has a higher total, the battle is a **draw**.

COALITION A
TERRITORY

COALITION B
TERRITORY

BATTLEPLAN
LAUNCH THE ATTACK

A mighty coalition has invaded rival lands, seeking blood and conquest. The defenders must work together to fight off these invaders.

COALITION OF DEATH
This is a battle for 3 or more players. Use the Coalition of Death rules from page 52.

THE ARMIES
The warlords roll off. The winner picks which coalition will be the Attacker coalition and which will be the Defender coalition.

OBJECTIVES
Set up 3 objectives as shown on the map.

SET-UP
The warlords roll off, and the winner decides which territory each coalition will use. The territories are shown on the map. The coalition of the warlord who won the roll-off sets up first. The opposing coalition sets up second. Units must be set up wholly within the coalition's own territory.

RESERVES
Should a player wish, any of their units may start the battle in reserve instead of being set up on the battlefield. Starting from the second battle round, reserve units can join the battle during any of their coalition's movement phases. All of the models in the unit must be set up within their coalition's territory, within 3" of the battlefield edge and more than 9" from any enemy units. This counts as their move for that movement phase.

GLORIOUS VICTORY
The coalition with the most victory points at the end of the battle wins a **major victory**. If both coalitions have the same number of victory points, use the tiebreaker to determine which coalition wins a **minor victory** or if the battle is a **draw**.

VICTORY POINTS
Victory points are scored as follows:

- Each time a coalition slays an enemy model that has a Wounds characteristic of 10 or more, that coalition scores 1 victory point.

- If a coalition slays an enemy general, that coalition scores 1 victory point. If that general was the enemy warlord's general, that coalition scores 1 extra victory point.

- At the end of each of their turns, the Defender coalition scores 1 victory point for each objective that they control and the Attacker coalition scores 2 victory points for each objective that they control.

TIEBREAKER
If the coalitions are tied on victory points at the end of the battle, each coalition must add up the points value of any enemy units that were destroyed during the battle (excluding any new units that were added to the armies after the battle started). If one coalition has a higher total, that coalition wins a **minor victory**. If neither coalition has a higher total, the battle is a **draw**.

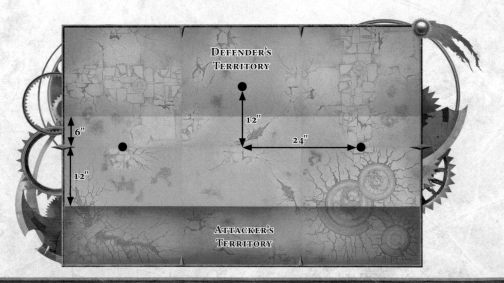

DEFENDER'S TERRITORY

12"

6"

24"

12"

ATTACKER'S TERRITORY

THE ANVIL OF APOTHEOSIS

In the vaults of high Sigmaron, the greatest warriors of the Stormcast Eternals are forged upon the Anvil of Apotheosis. Across the realms can be found similar champions of all races and allegiances, each having endured their own crucible of testing and each possessing quirks and qualities that have seen them rise to power.

The rules in this section will enable you to create a unique hero of your own design. This could be an existing Citadel Miniature that you wish to give its own bespoke rules or a conversion you have made. You will find examples of heroes made by members of the Design Studio over the next few pages to help spur your imagination.

There are 6 steps outlined in this section that you must follow to create your own hero. As you follow the steps, you will have a host of options to choose from, including powerful weapons and ferocious mounts. After completing all of the steps, you will be able to field your hero in your narrative play games of Age of Sigmar.

A blank warscroll to record your hero upon can be printed out from www.warhammer-community.com.

The 6 steps are as follows:

1. Set a destiny point limit for your hero.

2. Choose your hero's ancestry.

3. Equip your hero with weapons from the armoury.

4. Pick an archetype for your hero: Commander, Mage or Acolyte.

5. Choose a bestial companion (if any) for your hero.

6. Spend your remaining destiny points on any characteristic enhancements or abilities for your hero.

CHARACTERISTIC ENHANCEMENTS AND ABILITIES

Many of the steps include **options** to give your hero a [Characteristic Enhancement] or an [Ability]. If the option gives a [Characteristic Enhancement], modify the characteristic as noted. If it gives an [Ability], write the ability in the 'Abilities' section of your hero's warscroll. The same characteristic enhancement can be chosen up to 3 times for your hero; however, the same ability cannot be chosen more than once. Lastly, some options will have **restrictions** that limit which keywords can or cannot take a certain option.

STEP 1 – THE DESTINY POINT LIMIT

When creating your hero, the first step is to pick 1 of the following destiny point limits for your hero:

Champion
Limit: 20 destiny points

Conqueror
Limit: 40 destiny points

As you complete the rest of the steps, each option you pick for your hero will cost a certain number of **destiny points**. This will often be abbreviated as **DP**. Keep a running tally of the number of destiny points you have spent. The tally cannot exceed the limit you have set.

STEP 2 – ANCESTRIES

The second step is to pick the ancestry for your hero. There are 23 to choose from in total, from Aelf to Daemon to Stormcast Eternal and so forth. The ancestry you pick will cost a number of destiny points (as indicated in the upper-right corner of the ancestry) and will populate your hero's Move, Wounds, Bravery and Save characteristics. The ancestry will also give them a set of keywords. Write all of these down on your hero's warscroll after making your choice. If the ancestry includes the <army> keyword, you must pick 1 of the army keywords listed for that ancestry.

For example, when product developer Ben Johnson was creating his Khainite priestess, he began by picking the Champion destiny point limit (giving him 20 DP to spend) and then chose the Aelf ancestry. The Aelf ancestry costs 3 destiny points and includes the <army> keyword. Ben fittingly picked the 'Daughters of Khaine' army keyword for his hero.

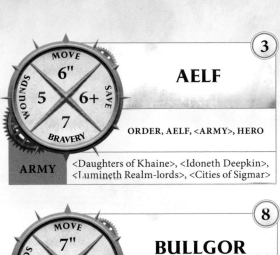

AELF

(3)

ORDER, AELF, <ARMY>, HERO

ARMY — <Daughters of Khaine>, <Idoneth Deepkin>, <Lumineth Realm-lords>, <Cities of Sigmar>

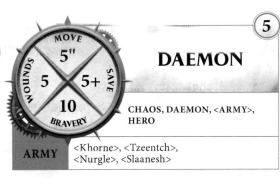

BONESPLITTER ORRUK

(3)

DESTRUCTION, ORRUK, ORRUK WARCLANS, BONESPLITTERZ, HERO

BULLGOR

(8)

CHAOS, BEASTS OF CHAOS, WARHERD, BULLGOR, HERO

DAEMON

(5)

CHAOS, DAEMON, <ARMY>, HERO

ARMY — <Khorne>, <Tzeentch>, <Nurgle>, <Slaanesh>

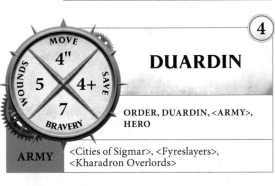

DEATHMAGE

(3)

DEATH, DEATHMAGE, HERO

This hero may be selected as part of a Grand Host of Nagash, Legion of Sacrament, Legion of Blood or Legion of Night army and gain the appropriate faction keyword.

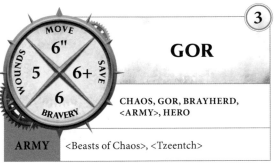

DRAGON OGOR

(10)

CHAOS, BEASTS OF CHAOS, THUNDERSCORN, DRAGON OGOR, HERO

DUARDIN

(4)

ORDER, DUARDIN, <ARMY>, HERO

ARMY — <Cities of Sigmar>, <Fyreslayers>, <Kharadron Overlords>

GOR

(3)

CHAOS, GOR, BRAYHERD, <ARMY>, HERO

ARMY — <Beasts of Chaos>, <Tzeentch>

GROT

(3)

DESTRUCTION, GROT, GLOOMSPITE GITZ, <ARMY>, HERO

ARMY — <Moonclan>, <Spiderfang>

HUMAN

(4)

ORDER, HUMAN, CITIES OF SIGMAR, HERO

IRONJAW ORRUK ⑤

MOVE	4"
WOUNDS	6
SAVE	5+
BRAVERY	7

DESTRUCTION, ORRUK,
ORRUK WARCLANS,
IRONJAWZ, HERO

MALIGNANT ⑫

MOVE	6"
WOUNDS	5
SAVE	4+
BRAVERY	10

DEATH, MALIGNANT,
NIGHTHAUNT, HERO

This hero comes with the 'Fly' and 'Ethereal' abilities (see later).

MORDANT ⑥

MOVE	6"
WOUNDS	6
SAVE	5+
BRAVERY	10

DEATH, MORDANT,
FLESH-EATER COURTS, HERO

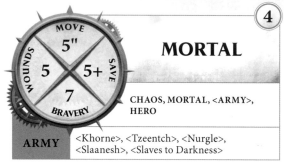

MORTAL ④

MOVE	5"
WOUNDS	5
SAVE	5+
BRAVERY	7

CHAOS, MORTAL, <ARMY>,
HERO

ARMY: <Khorne>, <Tzeentch>, <Nurgle>,
<Slaanesh>, <Slaves to Darkness>

OGOR ⑦

MOVE	6"
WOUNDS	7
SAVE	5+
BRAVERY	8

DESTRUCTION, OGOR,
OGOR MAWTRIBES,
<ARMY>, HERO

ARMY: <Beastclaw Raiders>, <Gutbusters>

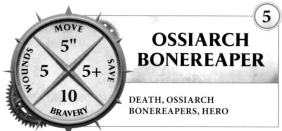

OSSIARCH BONEREAPER ⑤

MOVE	5"
WOUNDS	5
SAVE	5+
BRAVERY	10

DEATH, OSSIARCH
BONEREAPERS, HERO

SAURUS ⑥

MOVE	5"
WOUNDS	6
SAVE	4+
BRAVERY	8

ORDER, SERAPHON, SAURUS,
HERO

SKAVEN ③

MOVE	6"
WOUNDS	5
SAVE	6+
BRAVERY	6

CHAOS, SKAVEN, SKAVENTIDE,
<ARMY>, HERO

ARMY: <Masterclan>, <Clans Pestilens, Nurgle>,
<Clans Verminus>, <Clans Skryre>,
<Clans Moulder>, <Clans Eshin>

Dan Harden from White Dwarf built these two heroes. For the Skaven Arch-Warlock, Raticus-Klaue, he chose the Mage archetype and then spent the rest of his destiny points powering up Raticus's claw weapon to represent its warp-lightning charge.

This fearsome aelven Sorceress hails from the Realm of Metal and unleashes deadly flurries of eldritch blades upon her foes. To represent this, Dan gave her the Bow two-handed weapon, renamed the 'Quicksilver Swords'.

SKELETON

MOVE 4" | WOUNDS 5 | SAVE 6+ | BRAVERY 10

DEATH, SKELETON, DEATHRATTLE, HERO

This hero may be selected as part of a Grand Host of Nagash, Legion of Sacrament, Legion of Blood or Legion of Night army and gain the appropriate faction keyword.

SKINK

MOVE 8" | WOUNDS 4 | SAVE 6+ | BRAVERY 6

ORDER, SERAPHON, SKINK, HERO

VAMPIRE

MOVE 5" | WOUNDS 5 | SAVE 5+ | BRAVERY 10

DEATH, VAMPIRE, SOULBLIGHT, HERO

This hero may be selected as part of a Grand Host of Nagash, Legion of Sacrament, Legion of Blood or Legion of Night army and gain the appropriate faction keyword.

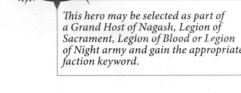

STORMCAST ETERNAL

MOVE 5" | WOUNDS 5 | SAVE 4+ | BRAVERY 8

ORDER, CELESTIAL, HUMAN, STORMCAST ETERNALS, HERO

SYLVANETH

MOVE 5" | WOUNDS 5 | SAVE 5+ | BRAVERY 7

ORDER, SYLVANETH, HERO

Rules writer James Gallagher made a mounted Wight King to lead his skeletal hordes. Starting with the Skeleton ancestry, he added a mounted beast and the 'Consummate Commander' ability to empower his minions.

Background writer Phil Kelly's 'Grunta Boss' regularly leads the heavy cavalry mobs of his Ironjawz into the best scraps. The 'Vicious Charge' ability is perfect for representing the savagery of a rampaging Gore-grunta.

STEP 3 – THE ARMOURY

The next step is to arm your hero with weapons from the armoury. A hero can be armed with 1 of the following weapon options:

- 1 one-handed melee weapon.
- 2 one-handed melee weapons.
- 1 one-handed melee weapon and a shield.
- 1 two-handed melee weapon.
- 1 Handbow and 1 one-handed melee weapon.
- 1 Bow and 1 one-handed melee weapon.

The weapon options and their profiles are listed in the table below, and each weapon option costs a number of destiny points as noted in the rightmost column of the table.

For each weapon chosen, add the profile to your hero's warscroll and write the name of the weapon in the description section. For added flavour, you may wish to personalise your weapons – for example, your hero's Sword could be named 'The Blade of Doom' or you could use the Handbow profile to represent an arcane zap or other ranged attack.

In step 6, you will be presented with options to improve your hero's weapons.

ONE-HANDED WEAPONS

MELEE WEAPONS	Range	Attacks	To Hit	To Wound	Rend	Damage	DP
Sword	1"	3	3+	4+	-	1	1
Axe	1"	3	4+	3+	-1	1	1
Hammer	1"	2	4+	3+	-1	2	1
Spear	2"	3	4+	4+	-	1	1
Unarmed Strike	1"	4	4+	4+	-	1	1
Flail	3"	2	4+	4+	-	1	1
Improvised Weapon	1"	3	4+	4+	-	1	0
MISSILE WEAPONS	**Range**	**Attacks**	**To Hit**	**To Wound**	**Rend**	**Damage**	**DP**
Handbow	9"	2	4+	4+	-	1	1

TWO-HANDED WEAPONS

MELEE WEAPONS	Range	Attacks	To Hit	To Wound	Rend	Damage	DP
Greatsword	1"	3	3+	3+	-1	2	2
Great Axe	1"	3	4+	2+	-2	2	2
Grandhammer	1"	2	4+	2+	-2	3	2
Great Spear	2"	3	4+	3+	-1	2	2
Mage's Staff	1"	3	4+	3+	-1	D3	1
Scythe	2"	4	4+	4+	-1	1	1
MISSILE WEAPONS	**Range**	**Attacks**	**To Hit**	**To Wound**	**Rend**	**Damage**	**DP**
Bow	18"	2	4+	4+	-	2	2

SHIELD

Restrictions: No MALIGNANT	[Characteristic Enhancement] Improve your hero's Save characteristic by 1	DP 2

STEP 4 – ARCHETYPES

Next, you need to pick 1 of the following archetypes for your hero and then any associated abilities. There are 3 archetypes to choose from: **Commander**, **Acolyte** or **Mage**. Each of these will unlock different types of abilities for your hero. Commanders have access to command abilities, Acolytes have access to prayers and Mages have access to spells. Archetypes do not cost any destiny points.

COMMANDER

Keywords: None

Restrictions: No DEATHMAGE or MASTERCLAN

[**Ability**] Pick 1 of the following command abilities and add it to your hero's warscroll.

Lead the Attack: You can use this command ability at the start of the combat phase. If you do so, pick 1 friendly unit wholly within 18" of this HERO. Add 1 to hit rolls for attacks made by that unit until the end of that phase.	**Lead the Defence:** You can use this command ability at the start of the combat phase. If you do so, pick 1 friendly unit wholly within 18" of this HERO. Add 1 to save rolls for attacks that target that unit until the end of that phase.

ACOLYTE

Keywords: PRIEST

Restrictions: No DAEMON, DEATHMAGE, SAURUS or SKAVEN (except CLANS PESTILENS)

[**Ability**] First, pick 1 of the prayers below. Then, add the following ability to your hero's warscroll, followed by the prayer you picked.

Divine Prayers: In your hero phase, this HERO can chant the following prayer. If they do so, make a prayer roll by rolling a dice. On a 1-2, the prayer is not answered. On a 3+, the prayer is answered.

Wrathful Invocation: If this prayer is answered, pick 1 enemy unit within 18" of this HERO. That unit suffers D3 mortal wounds.	***Shield of Faith:*** If this prayer is answered, pick 1 friendly unit wholly within 12" of this HERO. Until the start of your next hero phase, roll a dice each time a wound or mortal wound is allocated to that unit. On a 6, that wound or mortal wound is negated.

MAGE

Keywords: WIZARD

Restrictions: No DUARDIN, KHORNE or SAURUS

[**Ability**] Pick up to 1 spell from the Spell Table and add it to your hero's warscroll.

MAGIC

This HERO is a WIZARD. They can attempt to cast 1 spell in your hero phase and attempt to unbind 1 spell in the enemy hero phase. They know the Arcane Bolt and Mystic Shield spells. In addition, they know any spells you have picked for them from the Spell Table.

SPELL TABLE

Aura of Protection: Aura of Protection has a casting value of 7. If successfully cast, until the start of your next hero phase, roll a dice each time a wound or mortal wound is allocated to a friendly unit wholly within 12" of the caster. On a 6, that wound or mortal wound is negated.

Curse of Damnation: Curse of Damnation has a casting value of 7. If successfully cast, pick 1 enemy unit within 12" of the caster and visible to them. That unit suffers D3 mortal wounds. In addition, subtract 1 from save rolls for attacks that target that unit until the start of your next hero phase.

Wildfire: Wildfire has a casting value of 6. If successfully cast, pick 1 enemy unit. Roll 1 dice for each model in that unit that is within 12" of the caster and visible to them. For each 5+, that unit suffers 1 mortal wound. If that unit has only 1 model, roll 3 dice instead of 1.

Raise Dead: Raise Dead has a casting value of 6. If successfully cast, pick 1 friendly unit within 12" of the caster and visible to them. You may return a number of slain models that have a combined Wounds characteristic of D3 or less to that unit.

STEP 5 – BESTIAL COMPANION

In this step, you need to decide whether or not your hero will have a bestial companion. There are 3 types of bestial companion: **Minor Beast**, **Mounted Beast** and **Gargantuan Beast**. A hero can only ever have 1 bestial companion picked for them. A Minor Beast follows or guards your hero, such as Korghos Khul's Flesh Hound, Grizzlemaw. A Mounted Beast can be anything from a stallion to a Dracoline or Rot Fly. A Gargantuan Beast is a truly colossal mount, such as a dragon, Thundertusk or Manticore. If you do not want to choose a bestial companion for your hero, you can skip this step.

You can pick 1 of the following bestial companions. Each costs a number of destiny points as listed in the table.

MINOR BEAST

Restrictions: None		[Characteristic Enhancement] Add 1 to your hero's Wounds characteristic				DP 6
MELEE WEAPONS	Range	Attacks	To Hit	To Wound	Rend	Damage
Claws	1"	2	5+	5+	-	1
Maw	1"	1	4+	3+	-1	D3

Add the following text to your hero's description:

MINOR BEAST: This model's Minor Beast attacks with its Claws and Maw. For rules purposes, it is treated the same as a mount.

MOUNTED BEAST

Restrictions: No **Bullgor** or **Dragon Ogor**		[Characteristic Enhancement] Add 2 to your hero's Wounds characteristic Change your hero's Move characteristic to 8"				DP 8
MELEE WEAPONS	Range	Attacks	To Hit	To Wound	Rend	Damage
Claws	1"	2	5+	5+	-	1
Maw	1"	1	4+	3+	-1	D3

Add the following text to your hero's description:

MOUNT: This model's Mounted Beast attacks with its Claws and Maw.

GARGANTUAN BEAST

Restrictions: No **Bullgor** or **Dragon Ogor**		[Characteristic Enhancement] Add 8 to your hero's Wounds characteristic Change your hero's Move characteristic to ✷				DP 15
MELEE WEAPONS	Range	Attacks	To Hit	To Wound	Rend	Damage
Claws	2"	✷	4+	3+	-1	2
Maw	2"	2	3+	3+	-2	✷

Add the following text to your hero's description:

MOUNT: This model's Gargantuan Beast attacks with its Claws and Maw.

Add the following keywords to your hero's warscroll: **Monster**

Add the damage table on the right to your hero's warscroll.

DAMAGE TABLE			
Wounds Suffered	Move	Claws	Maw
0-3	10"	6	4
4-6	8"	5	3
7-9	6"	4	2
10-11	4"	3	1
12+	2"	2	1

If you have picked a bestial companion for your hero, you can pick any of the following options for them. Each option costs a number of destiny points as listed in the table.

BESTIAL COMPANION OPTIONS		
Winged Beast	[Ability] Add the following text to your hero's description: **FLY:** This model can fly. **Restrictions:** No Minor Beast	DP 4
Breath Attack	[Ability] **Breath Attack:** In your shooting phase, you can pick 1 enemy unit within 6" of this model. Roll a number of dice equal to the number of models from that enemy unit that are within 6" of this model. For each 6, that enemy unit suffers 1 mortal wound. **Restrictions:** Gargantuan Beast only	DP 4
Vicious Charge	[Ability] **Vicious Charge:** After this model makes a charge move, you can pick 1 enemy unit within 1" of this model and roll a dice. On a 2+, that enemy unit suffers D3 mortal wounds.	DP 1
Razor-sharp Claws	[Characteristic Enhancement] Improve the Rend characteristic of the bestial companion's Claws by 1 (to a maximum of -3).	DP 2
Poisonous Bite	[Ability] **Poisonous Bite:** If the unmodified hit roll for an attack made with the bestial companion's Maw is 6, that attack inflicts 1 mortal wound on the target in addition to any normal damage.	DP 2
Gobble Attack	[Ability] **Gobble Attack:** Each time this model attacks, after all of this model's attacks have been resolved, you can pick 1 enemy model within 1" of this model and roll a dice. If the roll is equal to or greater than that enemy model's Wounds characteristic, it is slain. **Restrictions:** Gargantuan Beast only	DP 3
Terror	[Ability] **Terror:** Subtract 1 from the Bravery characteristic of enemy units while they are within 3" of any friendly units with this ability. **Restrictions:** Gargantuan Beast only	DP 1
Savage Frenzy	[Characteristic Enhancement] Pick either the bestial companion's Claws or Maw. Add 1 to the Attacks characteristic of that weapon. For Gargantuan Beasts, add 1 to each row of the appropriate column in the damage table.	DP 1
Lashing Tail	[Ability] **Lashing Tail:** At the end of the combat phase, roll a dice for each enemy unit within 3" of this model. If the roll is less than the number of models in that unit, that unit suffers D3 mortal wounds. **Restrictions:** Gargantuan Beast only	DP 3
Savage Ferocity	[Characteristic Enhancement] Pick either the bestial companion's Claws or Maw. Improve the To Hit characteristic of that weapon by 1.	DP 1
Savage Strength	[Characteristic Enhancement] Pick either the bestial companion's Claws or Maw. Improve the To Wound characteristic of that weapon by 1.	DP 1
Stomp	[Ability] **Stomp:** At the end of the combat phase, you can pick 1 enemy unit within 1" of this unit and roll a dice. On a 2+, that enemy unit suffers D3 mortal wounds. **Restrictions:** Gargantuan Beast only	DP 2

STEP 6 – CHARACTERISTIC ENHANCEMENTS AND ABILITIES

The final step is to pick any other options for your hero. Each costs a number of destiny points as listed in the tables.

CHARACTERISTIC ENHANCEMENTS AND ABILITIES		
Superior Speed	[Characteristic Enhancement] Add 1 to your hero's Move characteristic.	DP 2
Superior Vitality	[Characteristic Enhancement] Add 1 to your hero's Wounds characteristic.	DP 1
Superior Leadership	[Characteristic Enhancement] Add 1 to your hero's Bravery characteristic.	DP 1
Extra Armour	[Characteristic Enhancement] Improve your hero's Save characteristic by 1 (to a maximum of 3+).	DP 2
Mighty Weapon	[Characteristic Enhancement] Pick 1 of your hero's weapons (not including mount weapons). Add 1 to the Damage characteristic of that weapon. Weapons that have a random Damage characteristic cannot be picked.	DP 2
Sharpened Edge	[Characteristic Enhancement] Pick 1 of your hero's weapons (not including mount weapons). Improve the Rend characteristic of that weapon by 1 (to a maximum of -3).	DP 2
Ethereal	[Ability] Ethereal: Ignore modifiers (positive or negative) when making save rolls for attacks that target this model.	DP 4
Ward	[Ability] Ward: Roll a dice each time a wound or mortal wound is allocated to this model. On a 6, that wound or mortal wound is negated.	DP 3
Fly	[Ability] Add the following text to your hero's description: **FLY:** This model can fly.	DP 4
Frenzy	[Ability] Frenzy: If the unmodified hit roll for an attack made with this model's melee weapons (not including mount weapons) is 6, that attack scores 2 hits on the target instead of 1. Make a wound and save roll for each hit.	DP 3
Regenerate	[Ability] Regenerate: In your hero phase, you can roll a dice for this model. If you do so, on a 4+, heal up to D3 wounds allocated to this model.	DP 3
Battle Standard Bearer	[Characteristic Enhancement] This model gains the TOTEM keyword.	DP 1

CHARACTERISTIC ENHANCEMENTS AND ABILITIES		
Inspiring	[Ability] Inspiring: While friendly units are wholly within 12" of this model, they can use this model's Bravery characteristic instead their own. Increase the range of this ability to 18" if this model is a TOTEM.	DP 1
Weapon Master	[Characteristic Enhancement] Pick 1 of your hero's weapons (not including mount weapons). Improve the To Hit characteristic of that weapon by 1.	DP 2
Superior Strength	[Characteristic Enhancement] Pick 1 of your hero's weapons (not including mount weapons). Improve the To Wound characteristic of that weapon by 1.	DP 2
Ferocity	[Characteristic Enhancement] Pick 1 of your hero's weapons (not including mount weapons). Add 1 to the Attacks characteristic of that weapon.	DP 2
Consummate Commander	[Ability] Consummate Commander: If this model is part of your army, at the start of the first battle round, you receive 1 extra command point.	DP 5
Archmage	[Ability] Archmage: Add 1 to casting and unbinding rolls for this model. Restrictions: WIZARD only	DP 3
Arch-priest	[Ability] Arch-priest: Add 1 to prayer rolls for this model. Restrictions: PRIEST only	DP 3
Zealot	[Ability] Zealot: This model can run and still charge in the same turn.	DP 4
Decapitating Strike	[Ability] Decapitating Strike: If the unmodified wound roll for an attack made with this model's melee weapons (not including mount weapons) is 6, that attack inflicts 1 mortal wound on the target in addition to any normal damage.	DP 4
Deadeye	[Ability] Deadeye: If the unmodified hit roll for an attack made with this model's missile weapons (not including mount weapons) is 6, that attack inflicts 1 mortal wound on the target in addition to any normal damage.	DP 4

USING YOUR HERO IN BATTLE

Once you have created your hero, you are ready to field them in narrative play battles. Below are a number of ideas of how to incorporate your hero into your games of Age of Sigmar.

Campaign Games: If you are playing a campaign (such as the Whisper Engine campaign featured on pages 48-51), you could agree that after each battle, players accrue D3 destiny points with which to improve their hero.

Open Play Games: With your opponent's permission, if you are using the Open War army generator (pg 122-125), your hero can be picked to be a Champion or Conqueror in your army depending on the destiny point limit for that hero.

Matched Play Games: Using these heroes in matched play is strictly a house rule and requires your opponent's permission. If you do so, count the number of destiny points you have spent on your hero and multiply the total by 10. This is the Pitched Battle points cost of that hero. In addition, your hero has the Leader battlefield role, unless it has the **MONSTER** keyword, in which case it has the Leader and Behemoth battlefield roles.

Army painter Jay Goldfinch built this terrifying Herald of Khorne on Bloodcrusher. To turn its flame-wreathed hellblade into a truly fearsome weapon, Jay gave it the 'Mighty Weapon' option three times, for a total of 4 damage inflicted with each successful wound!

Dan Harden converted this Weirdnob Shaman to represent an orruk champion from the Realm of Shadow. No doubt he'll have all manner of kunnin' tricks up his sleeve; he might have been given options such as 'Ward' or 'Superior Speed' – or maybe even 'Fly'!

This Barrow Banshee was converted by studio artist Thomas Elliott. The shield is just for visual effect (as this hero is already 'Ethereal'). Thomas used the Handbow missile weapon to represent the Banshee's soul-shredding scream, fittingly renamed 'Death Shriek'.

This noble knight of the Stormcast Eternals was made by Ben Johnson. Ben focused on making this hero into a powerful battlefield leader by giving them the 'Superior Leadership', 'Inspiring' and 'Consummate Commander' options.

James Gallagher chose the 'Regenerate' ability to represent this Soulblight noble's vampyric nature, and although the model has no visible wings, James gave her the 'Fly' ability – perhaps she uses magical mists or transforms into a bat!

Thaxgor Ruin is the latest champion of rules writer Sam Pearson's Blades of Khorne army. The Acolyte archetype was chosen to give Thaxgor the Priest keyword, and the prayer 'Wrathful Invocation' is well suited to represent the Blood God's fury!

This impressive Vampire Lord is the leader of Thomas Elliott's Legion of Blood. The colossal creature upon which the Vampire rides is represented by a Gargantuan Beast with the 'Breath Attack', 'Terror' and 'Winged Beast' options, allowing it to strike fear into any foe.

MATCHED
PLAY GAMES

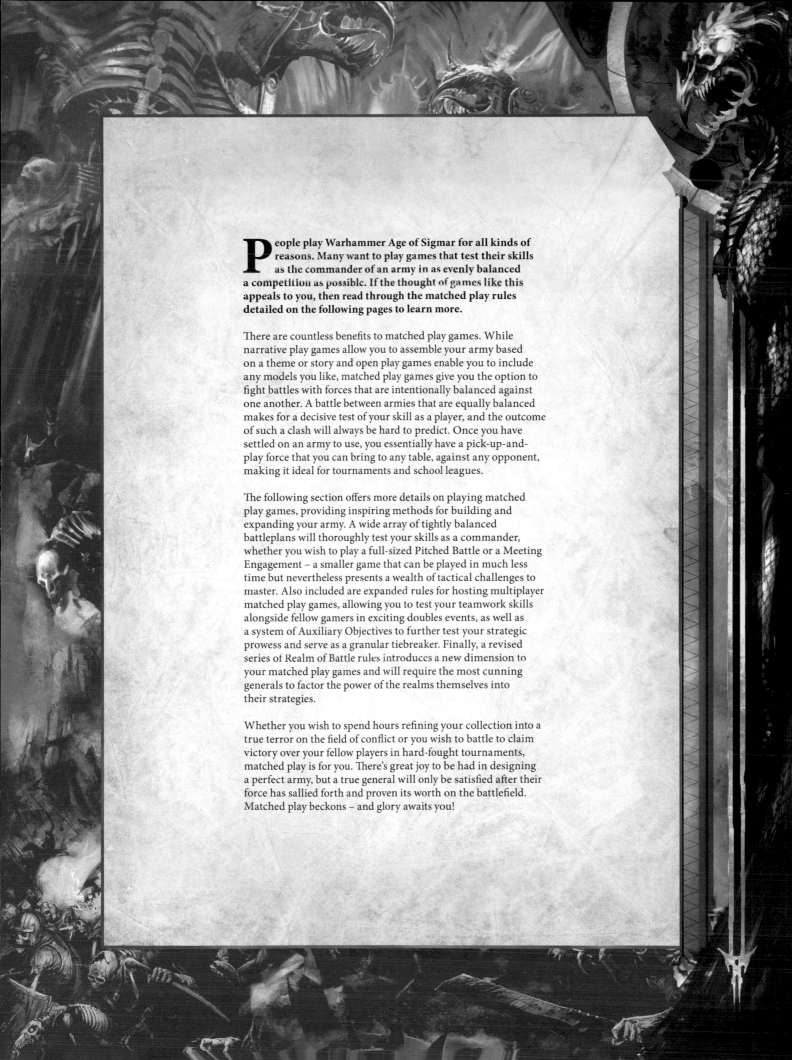

People play Warhammer Age of Sigmar for all kinds of reasons. Many want to play games that test their skills as the commander of an army in as evenly balanced a competition as possible. If the thought of games like this appeals to you, then read through the matched play rules detailed on the following pages to learn more.

There are countless benefits to matched play games. While narrative play games allow you to assemble your army based on a theme or story and open play games enable you to include any models you like, matched play games give you the option to fight battles with forces that are intentionally balanced against one another. A battle between armies that are equally balanced makes for a decisive test of your skill as a player, and the outcome of such a clash will always be hard to predict. Once you have settled on an army to use, you essentially have a pick-up-and-play force that you can bring to any table, against any opponent, making it ideal for tournaments and school leagues.

The following section offers more details on playing matched play games, providing inspiring methods for building and expanding your army. A wide array of tightly balanced battleplans will thoroughly test your skills as a commander, whether you wish to play a full-sized Pitched Battle or a Meeting Engagement – a smaller game that can be played in much less time but nevertheless presents a wealth of tactical challenges to master. Also included are expanded rules for hosting multiplayer matched play games, allowing you to test your teamwork skills alongside fellow gamers in exciting doubles events, as well as a system of Auxiliary Objectives to further test your strategic prowess and serve as a granular tiebreaker. Finally, a revised series of Realm of Battle rules introduces a new dimension to your matched play games and will require the most cunning generals to factor the power of the realms themselves into their strategies.

Whether you wish to spend hours refining your collection into a true terror on the field of conflict or you wish to battle to claim victory over your fellow players in hard-fought tournaments, matched play is for you. There's great joy to be had in designing a perfect army, but a true general will only be satisfied after their force has sallied forth and proven its worth on the battlefield. Matched play beckons – and glory awaits you!

INTRODUCING MATCHED PLAY

In the Mortal Realms, armies come in all shapes and sizes, each with their unique strengths and weaknesses. To truly test a general's mettle as a commander, there needs to be a level playing field that accounts for the variety of forces abroad in the Age of Sigmar. This is the goal of matched play.

The main differences between matched play and open play lie in army selection and battleplan design. Matched play games include rules that allow players to pick armies of equal power, and the battleplans used in matched play games are designed to provide tactically challenging games where each side has a more-or-less equal chance of winning.

The emphasis of matched play gaming is on planning, tactics and military cunning, so it is the perfect format for those who wish to test their skill as strategists and commanders. While narrative and open play games can vary greatly in scope and content, presenting you with all manner of scenarios to battle through, matched play games are all about you and your army, the models you select and the tactics you use. They are driven by every player's desire for a satisfying and well-earned victory.

MATCHED PLAY RULES
Three types of matched play game are featured in this section – Pitched Battle, Meeting Engagement and Coalition of Death. The Pitched Battle rules are intended to provide

as even a playing field as possible, ensuring that armies are equally matched and victory conditions are clear while offering no advantage to either side. A Pitched Battle is the ideal place to start when playing matched play games, and these rules are the most commonly used in tournaments the world over.

Meeting Engagements build on the precedent set by the Pitched Battle rules but are designed to enable you to play matched play games on a smaller battlefield. This makes them ideal for competitors with limited time and space. In this system, armies come onto the battlefield in waves, each contingent arriving at a different time to try and turn the course of the battle.

Finally, Coalition of Death allows you to fight multiplayer battles by joining forces with a fellow player. These are great for doubles events and will force you to master tag-team strategising to come out on top.

MATCHED PLAY ARMIES
Pitched Battle, Meeting Engagement and Coalition of Death games all use Pitched Battle profiles, which assign a minimum and maximum

size for each unit as well as a points cost you have to spend in order to include that unit in your army. The profiles for all available units can be found in the *Pitched Battle Profiles 2020* booklet that accompanies this volume, for ease of use when building your army.

Using this system, you and your opponent can assemble your armies based on a prearranged total of points so as to ensure that your forces are as equally matched as possible. Note that you can use these profiles in any kind of game, not just those featured in this section.

There are other methods of choosing an army that don't involve adding up points but still suit the matched play format. For example, you could use the Wounds characteristics listed on each unit's warscroll as a guideline, either setting an upper limit for the number of wounds a unit can have or a fixed total of wounds that an army can have as a whole.

Whichever method you use, assembling an army for a matched play game is an important part of the process, and an interesting challenge in its own right. Do you spend a lot of points on one high-powered

Warhammer Age of Sigmar tournaments are fantastic fun. Typically using the matched play format, they allow gamers to test their skills against one another in a series of competitive games.

model and risk being overrun by a larger force? Do you allocate your points evenly on a versatile middleweight force? Your knowledge of the units available to you will be pivotal, and understanding your opponent's forces can be just as vital. Making these choices may seem difficult at first, but once you've found the perfect formula, you'll be able to use it again and again to great effect, and this in turn can guide you when expanding your collection.

MATCHED PLAY BATTLEPLANS

This section includes 18 battleplans, 12 for use with the Pitched Battle rules (pg 72-75) and 6 for use with the Meeting Engagement rules (pg 88-91). Compared to open play and narrative play battleplans,

matched play battleplans tend to be quite simple in format, following a formula that ensures that the contest between the two players will be as even as possible. Such battleplans are typically fought to control one or more objectives, with victory points being earned to determine the overall winner. Destroying an opponent's units can, in some scenarios, offer an additional source of victory points or can occasionally be the focus of a battleplan. Either way, the victory conditions will usually be the same for both sides (a process known as **mirroring**), so that both players will be working towards the same objective.

The overall effect of this is a format that is ideal for 'pick-up' games between two players who have not met each other before. Matched

play battleplans allow a player to go ahead and collect an army, choosing whichever models they like within the constraints of the chosen rules, and then simply turn up at a club or gaming event, find an opponent and play!

GAMING CLUBS

A wonderful feature of the Games Workshop hobby is the degree to which it enables collectors to socialise. Hobbyists can connect via organised clubs, meet up, make friends and play games in a friendly and supportive environment. The Internet makes this process easier than ever, especially for those who can't easily get to a Games Workshop store – just search for 'Warhammer clubs' in your area to see what is available.

TOURNAMENTS

Throughout the wargaming hobby world, gaming events and tournaments take place virtually every weekend. Wherever you are, you're likely to find a tournament you can get to, and they're well worth attending. Not only will you get to meet up with a warm and welcoming community of fellow hobbyists, but you'll get to play some great games and see some truly amazing-looking armies. The internet is a great tool here – simply search for 'Warhammer Age of Sigmar tournaments' in your area and get ready to go to war.

Later in this book, you will find detailed information on how to take part in, or even run, a Warhammer Age of Sigmar tournament. Tournaments take place right around the world, every week of the year. Many of them are held at Warhammer World or are organised by games stores, while others are the heroic work of local gaming clubs. In many of these tournaments, the organisers will create exclusive, event-specific battleplans and rules sets. Regardless of whether the tournament you play sticks to the rules presented in this book or incorporates its own bespoke rules, it's sure to be an exciting competition and a rewarding hobby experience.

In a Warhammer Age of Sigmar tournament, you will play a series of games – either 3 or 5 depending on how long the tournament is intended to last – and you will score points depending on how well you do in each of your battles. Points are also awarded during the event based on how well painted your army is and how sporting an opponent you are. After the final round, the points that the players have scored will be added up, and whoever has scored the most will be declared the winner.

The aim of a Warhammer Age of Sigmar tournament is to measure your prowess as an all-round hobbyist, rather than just your ability to win games. In this, it reflects all aspects of the hobby and celebrates them all!

TOURNAMENT FORMAT

A Warhammer Age of Sigmar tournament consists of a number of rounds, with each player fighting 1 battle per round. Long tournaments will consist of 5 rounds (usually over two days), while short tournaments will consist of 3 rounds. The tournament will use typically the Pitched Battle, Meeting Engagement or Coalition of Death matched play rules presented in this book, plus whatever house rules are in effect.

THE RULES PACK

If you attend a tournament, the organisers will send you a rules pack. This will let you know how many rounds there will be, how long each round is and if any special rules apply to the games being played at the event. You can find an example rules pack for a Pitched Battle tournament on pages 112-113, a Meeting Engagement tournament on pages 114-115 and a Coalition of Death tournament on pages 116-117. This edition also includes rules and an example rules pack for Team Format tournaments involving teams of 4 players (pg 118-121).

If you decide to organise a tournament, feel free to change things in your rules pack to suit your own tastes and the tastes of your players. For example, you might want to run a tournament that awards extra points for extremely well-painted armies, or you may want to use battleplans you have written yourself, and so on. It would be a boring world indeed if every Warhammer Age of Sigmar tournament was exactly the same!

PITCHED BATTLES (2020)

The following rules allow you to play a Pitched Battle, either as a one-off game or as part of a tournament. They replace the Pitched Battle rules in the *General's Handbook 2019* and the *Warhammer Age of Sigmar Core Book*.

To play a Pitched Battle, you and your opponent will first need to decide what type of Pitched Battle game you want to fight, and then you will need to pick your armies. The type of game you pick will determine how big the battle will be – the larger the battle, the more points you will have to spend on units for your army but the longer the game will take.

There are three different types of Pitched Battle to choose from:

Game Type	Game Length
Vanguard	Up to 1 ½ hours
Battlehost	2 to 2 ½ hours
Warhost	3 or more hours

After you have agreed what type of game you want to play, look it up on the chart to the right. The chart lists the number of points each player has to spend on units for their army and what limitations apply to the types of unit that players can bring. Each player must pick the units they will use for their army as described next.

SPECIAL RULE
The following rule applies to all matched play games:

You cannot make more than 1 dice roll (excluding re-rolls) to negate a wound or mortal wound that has been allocated to a model. If you could use more than one ability to negate allocated wounds or mortal wounds, you must pick which ability you will use.

PICKING YOUR ARMY
Each unit in a Pitched Battle is assigned a points value and a minimum and maximum unit size in its Pitched Battle profile. These profiles can be found in the *Pitched Battle Profiles 2020* book, on the Warhammer Community website or in the battletome where the warscroll for the unit appears.

PITCHED BATTLE CHART

	Vanguard	Battlehost	Warhost
Points	≤ 1,000	≤ 2,000	≤ 2,500
Leader	1-4	1-6	1-8
Battleline	2+	3+	4+
Artillery	0-2	0-4	0-5
Behemoth	0-2	0-4	0-5
Endless spells	0-2	0-3	0-4
Other units	Any number	Any number	Any number
Allied units (pts)	≤ 200	≤ 400	≤ 500

The game type you have chosen for your battle determines how many points you can spend on the units in your army. The combined points of the units in your army must not exceed the number of points shown on the chart. For example, in a Battlehost game, you can each field up to 2,000 points' worth of units.

ALLEGIANCE
In a Pitched Battle, you must pick an allegiance for your army as described in the core rules. All of the units in the army must either have that allegiance or be allied to that allegiance (see Allied Units).

ENDLESS SPELLS
Endless spells have Pitched Battle profiles and a points cost. By paying the spell's points cost, all **WIZARDS** in the player's army know that endless spell, and the player can use (and re-use) 1 endless spell model of the appropriate type in the battle. A player cannot take the same endless spell model more than once for their army (for example, you could not take 2 Balewind Vortex models).

BATTLEFIELD ROLES
Some units are assigned a battlefield role in their Pitched Battle profile. A unit's battlefield role is based on how it is used in a battle. The Pitched Battle chart above lists the minimum number of Leaders and Battleline

units you must include in a Pitched Battle army and the maximum number of Leaders, Behemoths, Artillery units and endless spells it can include. A model that is a Leader and a Behemoth counts as 1 Leader and 1 Behemoth in your army.

ALLIED UNITS
In a Pitched Battle, the number of points that can be spent on allies from the player's total points allowance is shown on the Pitched Battle chart above. For example, a player playing a Battlehost game can spend up to 400 of their 2,000 points on allied units. 1 in every 4 units in an army can be an allied unit.

Allied units are not included when working out the number of Battleline units in the army. They do count towards the maximum number of Leaders, Behemoths and Artillery units that can be included in an army.

WARSCROLL BATTALIONS
If a player's army includes the units needed to field a warscroll battalion, then the player can include the battalion as part of their army by paying the points cost for it as shown on its Pitched Battle profile. You must pay the cost of the units in the battalion as normal – the points value listed for each battalion is an extra cost that allows you to use it.

COMMAND POINTS

You can purchase up to 1 extra command point for 50 points. Add the extra command point to the command points you receive at the start of the battle.

ARMY ROSTER

Once you have picked your army, record the details on a piece of paper (your army roster) and show it to your opponent before setting up your army at the start of the battle.

The roster must include a list of the units, warscroll battalions and endless spells included in your army; what size the units are; the army's allegiance, which units are allies; if you have purchased an extra command point; and which model is the army's general. Use the notes column for each unit to record the command models you have chosen for it, the spells that are known by the **WIZARDS** in your army, any artefacts or other items wielded by **HEROES** in your army, and what command trait you have chosen for your general.

In a Pitched Battle, your general must be a Leader and cannot be an ally. If your general is slain in a Pitched Battle, do not pick a new one.

If your army includes any units that are given keywords when they are set up, such as units with a Mark of Chaos, these must be written down when the unit is added to the roster.

An example Pitched Battle roster can be found in the *Pitched Battle Profiles 2020* book.

PITCHED BATTLE BATTLEPLANS

We have provided 12 battleplans designed for use in Pitched Battles. Each offers a unique set of tactical challenges and will provide each player with a chance to show their skill. Before setting up the battlefield, pick a battleplan: first roll a D3 to determine which of the three tables opposite you will use, then roll a dice and consult the relevant table. The battleplans in Battleplan Table 1 are located in the *Warhammer Age of Sigmar Core Book*.

AUXILIARY OBJECTIVES

Auxiliary Objectives are secondary goals that represent the ulterior motives of the armies fighting a battle. Achieving your army's Auxiliary Objectives can turn a drawn battle into a victory. The rules for how to use Auxiliary Objectives can be found on pages 108-109.

D6	Battleplan Table 1
1	Blood and Glory
2	Escalation
3	Border War
4	Three Places of Power
5	Gifts from the Heavens
6	Take and Hold

D6	Battleplan Table 2
1	Knife to the Heart (pg 76)
2	Total Conquest (pg 77)
3	Battle for the Pass (pg 78)
4	Starstrike (pg 79)
5	Scorched Earth (pg 80)
6	Focal Points (pg 81)

D6	Battleplan Table 3
1	The Better Part of Valour (pg 82)
2	Shifting Objectives (pg 83)
3	Places of Arcane Power (pg 84)
4	The Blade's Edge (pg 85)
5	Total Commitment (pg 86)
6	Forcing the Hand (pg 87)

2019 BATTLEPLANS (OPTIONAL)

If either player in a Pitched Battle game has the 2019 edition of the *General's Handbook*, after determining which battleplan is to be used, one player can roll a dice to see if the battleplan with the same name from the *General's Handbook 2019* will be used instead of the version in the *General's Handbook 2020*.

If they decide to do so, on a 1-3, the battleplan to be used comes from the *General's Handbook 2019*, and on a 4-6, it comes from the *General's Handbook 2020*.

BATTLEFIELDS

A Pitched Battle is fought on a battlefield that measures 48" by 72". After deciding which battleplan is to be used, the players must first set up the objective markers and then the terrain features for the battle on the battlefield. The players can then proceed to set up their armies.

The location of any objectives can be found on the battleplan that is being used. After the objectives have been placed, each player must pick 5 terrain features from the lists to the right – 3 from the primary list and 2 from the secondary list.

The players then roll off, with the winner deciding who will be Player A and who will be Player B in the battle. Player A then sets up all of the terrain features on the battlefield. Terrain features must be set up more than 3" from the edge of the battlefield, more than 3" from any objectives and more than 6" from any other terrain features. Sometimes this will make it impossible for a terrain feature to be set up; in this case, it is not used.

After Player A has set up the terrain features for the battle, they must generate a scenery rule for any unique terrain features (if any). After scenery rules have been generated, Player B decides which territory each player will use. The players can then set up their armies as described in the battleplan they are using, starting with Player A.

FACTION TERRAIN

Sometimes the allegiance abilities for an army will allow it to include 1 or more terrain features, or a warscroll will allow you to set up 1 or more terrain features once the battle has begun. These are set up in addition to the terrain features that have been set up as previously described.

In a Pitched Battle, faction terrain must be set up more than 3" from any other terrain features and more than 1" from any objectives, in addition to any other restrictions that apply. Sometimes this will make it impossible for a faction terrain piece to be set up; in this case, it is not used.

SCENERY RULES

In a Pitched Battle, you must use the Scenery table opposite to randomly generate a scenery rule for each unique terrain feature. A terrain feature is **unique** if it is not included in the terrain lists above, even if it has a warscroll.

Roll a dice to determine which table will be used for the battle (1-3 = Table A; 4-6 = Table B), then roll for all unique terrain features on the battlefield from the same table.

COMMAND ABILITIES

In a Pitched Battle, you can use the following command abilities in addition to any others you can use.

All-out Attack: You can use this command ability at the start of the combat phase. If you do so, pick 1 friendly unit wholly within 12" of a friendly **HERO**, or wholly within 18" of a friendly **HERO** that is a general. You can re-roll hit rolls of 1 for attacks made by that unit until the end of that phase.

All-out Defence: You can use this command ability at the start of the combat phase. If you do so, pick 1 friendly unit that is wholly within 12" of a friendly **HERO**, or wholly within 18" of a friendly **HERO** that is a general. You can re-roll save rolls of 1 for attacks that target that unit until the end of that phase.

TERRAIN: PRIMARY LIST	
Azyrite Ruins	Azyrite Townscape Refuge
Azyrite Townscape Edifice	Numinous Occulum
Ophidian Archway	Sigmarite Mausoleum
Shattered Temple (single terrain feature that counts as 2 for the purpose of picking terrain features)	Sigmarite Dais (single terrain feature that counts as 2 for the purpose of picking terrain features)
Warcry Belltower	Wyldwood
Unique: Any other terrain feature that is no more than 10" across at its widest point and no more than 18" tall at its tallest point.	

TERRAIN: SECONDARY LIST	
Baleful Realmgate	Timeworn Ruins (consisting of 3 models instead of 10)
Walls and Fences (consisting of 2 models)	Warcry Statue Head
Warcry Barricades	Warcry Ruin
Unique: Any other terrain feature that is no more than 6" across at its widest point and no more than 6" tall at its tallest point.	

BATTLEFIELDS AT EVENTS

Some events, such as tournaments, will have battlefields with terrain features that have been set up before both players arrive at the table, or the position of terrain features may have been pre-determined by a third party. If this is the case, the players roll off to determine which territory each player will use, instead of using the battlefield set-up instructions described above.

If a faction terrain feature must be set up before any other terrain features, and the battlefield has already been set up by a third party, set up that faction terrain feature immediately before territories are determined.

Volley Fire: You can use this command ability at the start of your shooting phase. If you do so, pick 1 friendly unit that is wholly within 12" of a friendly **Hero**, or wholly within 18" of a friendly **Hero** that is a general. You can re-roll hit rolls of 1 for attacks made by that unit until the end of that phase.

At the Double: You can use this command ability after you make a run roll for a friendly unit that is within 6" of a friendly **Hero**, or within 12" of a friendly **Hero** that is a general. If you do so, the run roll is treated as being a 6.

Forward to Victory: You can use this command ability after you make a charge roll for a friendly unit that is within 6" of a friendly **Hero**, or within 12" of a friendly **Hero** that

is a general. If you do so, re-roll the charge roll.

Inspiring Presence: You can use this command ability at the start of the battleshock phase. If you do so, pick 1 friendly unit that is within 6" of friendly **Hero**, or within 12" of a friendly **Hero** that is a general. That unit does not have to take battleshock tests in that phase.

TRIUMPHS

In a Pitched Battle, you must use the following Triumph table instead of the one in the core rules. In addition, do not roll on this Triumph table if you won your last battle. Instead, after set-up is complete but before the first turn of the first battle round begins, the player who spent fewer points when selecting their army can roll on this Triumph table.

D3	Triumph
1	**Inspired:** Once per battle, when a friendly unit is picked to shoot or fight, you can say it is inspired. If you do so, you can re-roll hit rolls for attacks made by that unit until the end of that phase.
2	**Bloodthirsty:** Once per battle, when a friendly unit is picked to shoot or fight, you can say it is bloodthirsty. If you do so, you can re-roll wound rolls for attacks made by that unit until the end of that phase.
3	**Indomitable:** Once per battle, before you make a save roll for a friendly unit, you can say it is indomitable. If you do so, you can re-roll save rolls for attacks that target that unit until the end of that phase.

SCENERY TABLE		
Table A (1-3)		**Table B (4-6)**
D6	**Scenery Rule**	**D6**	**Scenery Rule**

D6	Scenery Rule (Table A)	D6	Scenery Rule (Table B)
1	**Damned:** At the start of your hero phase, you can pick one friendly unit within 1" of a Damned terrain feature to make a sacrifice. If you do so, that unit suffers D3 mortal wounds, but you can re-roll hit rolls of 1 for it until your next hero phase.	1	**Overgrown:** Models are not visible to each other if an imaginary straight line 1mm wide drawn between the closest points of the two models crosses over more than 1" of any Overgrown terrain features. This scenery rule does not apply if either model can fly.
2	**Arcane:** Add 1 to casting, unbinding and dispelling rolls for **Wizards** while they are within 1" of any Arcane terrain features.	2	**Entangling:** Subtract 2 from run and charge rolls (to a minimum of 0) for units that are within 1" of any Entangling terrain features.
3	**Inspiring:** Add 1 to the Bravery characteristic of units while they are within 1" of any Inspiring terrain features.	3	**Volcanic:** At the start of each hero phase, roll a dice for each Volcanic terrain feature. On a 6, each unit within 1" of that terrain feature suffers D3 mortal wounds.
4	**Deadly:** Roll a dice for each unit that finishes a normal move or charge move within 1" of any Deadly terrain features. On a 1, that unit suffers D3 mortal wounds.	4	**Commanding:** At the start of your hero phase, if your general and no enemy general is within 1" of any Commanding terrain features, add 1 to the number of command points you receive that hero phase.
5	**Mystical:** Roll a dice each time you allocate a wound or mortal wound to a model within 1" of any Mystical terrain features. On a 6+, the wound or mortal wound is negated.	5	**Healing:** At the start of your hero phase, roll a dice for each friendly unit that is within 1" of any Healing terrain features. On a 6, you can heal D3 wounds allocated to that unit.
6	**Sinister:** Subtract 1 from the Bravery characteristic of units while they are within 1" of any Sinister terrain features.	6	**Nullification:** In the enemy hero phase, if any **Heroes** from your army are within 1" of any Nullification terrain features, 1 of them can attempt to unbind 1 spell in the same manner as a **Wizard**. If they can already unbind spells, they can attempt to unbind 1 additional spell. In addition, an endless spell that is set up or finishes a move within 1" of any Nullification terrain features is dispelled.

BATTLEPLAN
KNIFE TO THE HEART

2020

Two warlords are each struggling to gain control of a vital objective that lies deep in their opponent's territory. Both must strive to capture their objective first, ruthlessly wiping out any enemy incursions into their own territory while pushing their own forces deep into the enemy's heartland.

PITCHED BATTLE
Use the Pitched Battle rules from pages 72-75.

OBJECTIVES
Set up 2 objectives, 1 objective in each half of the battlefield, as shown on the map.

SET-UP
The players alternate setting up units one at a time, starting with Player A. Players must set up units wholly within their own territory. The territories are shown on the map.

Continue to set up units until both players have set up their armies. If one player finishes first, the opposing player sets up the rest of the units in their army, one after another.

BATTLE LENGTH
The battle lasts for 5 battle rounds (or until the amount of time allocated for the battle runs out).

GLORIOUS VICTORY
Starting from the third battle round, one player immediately wins a **major victory** if they have control of both objectives.

If neither player has won a **major victory** by the end of battle, each player checks to see how many of their Auxiliary Objectives they have completed. If one player has completed more Auxiliary Objectives than their opponent, they win a **minor victory**. If both players have completed the same number of Auxiliary Objectives, the battle is a **draw**.

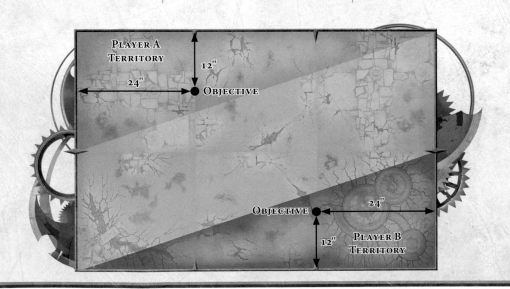

PLAYER A
TERRITORY

12"

24" ●— OBJECTIVE

OBJECTIVE ●

24"

12"

PLAYER B
TERRITORY

BATTLEPLAN
TOTAL CONQUEST

A blood-soaked battlefield is located at a vitally strategic site. Two armies stand upon this field of death, determined to drive their enemies from it and achieve total domination.

PITCHED BATTLE
Use the Pitched Battle rules from pages 72-75.

OBJECTIVES
Set up 4 objectives, 1 objective in each quarter of the battlefield, as shown on the map.

SET-UP
The players alternate setting up units one at a time, starting with Player A. Players must set up units wholly within their own territory and more than 9" from enemy territory. The territories are shown on the map.

Continue to set up units until both players have set up their armies. If one player finishes first, the opposing player sets up the rest of the units in their army, one after another.

BATTLE LENGTH
The battle lasts for 5 battle rounds (or until the amount of time allocated for the battle runs out).

GLORIOUS VICTORY
The player with the most victory points at the end of the battle wins a **major victory**.

If the players are tied on victory points at the end of the battle, each player checks to see how many of their Auxiliary Objectives they have completed. If one player has completed more Auxiliary Objectives than their opponent, they win a **minor victory**. If both players have completed the same number of Auxiliary Objectives, the battle is a **draw**.

VICTORY POINTS
Each player scores victory points at the end of each of their turns as follows:

- Each player scores 1 victory point for each objective they control.

- For each objective the player gained control of that turn that was previously controlled by their opponent, that player scores 1 additional victory point.

- If a player controls an objective while there is a friendly Leader unit within 6" of it, they score 1 additional victory point.

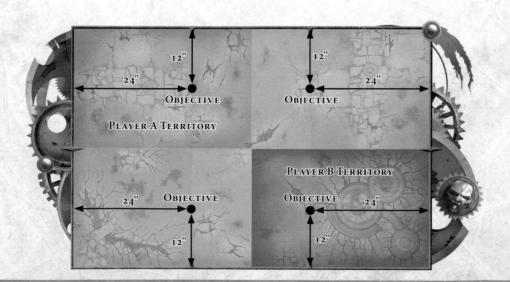

BATTLEPLAN
BATTLE FOR THE PASS

Many kingdoms in the Mortal Realms are separated by towering mountain ranges that can only be navigated by traversing a narrow pass. These defiles are of vital strategic importance, and many blood battles are fought over their control.

PITCHED BATTLE
Use the Pitched Battle rules from pages 72-75.

OBJECTIVES
Set up 4 objectives, 1 objective halfway between the centre of the battlefield and each battlefield edge, as shown on the map.

SET-UP
The players alternate setting up units one at a time, starting with Player A. Players must set up units wholly within their own territory. The territories are shown on the map.

Continue to set up units until both players have set up their armies. If one player finishes first, the opposing player sets up the rest of the units in their army, one after another.

BATTLE LENGTH
The battle lasts for 5 battle rounds (or until the amount of time allocated for the battle runs out).

GLORIOUS VICTORY
The player with the most victory points at the end of the battle wins a **major victory**.

If the players are tied on victory points at the end of the battle, each player checks to see how many of their Auxiliary Objectives they have completed. If one player has completed more Auxiliary Objectives than their opponent, they win a **minor victory**. If both players have completed the same number of Auxiliary Objectives, the battle is a **draw**.

VICTORY POINTS
Each player scores victory points at the end of each of their turns as follows:

- If a player controls the objective in their own territory, they score 1 victory point.

- For each objective the player controls that is not in either player's territory, they score 2 victory points.

- If a player controls the objective in their opponent's territory, they score 4 victory points.

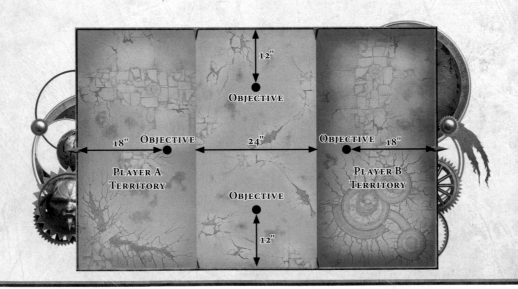

BATTLEPLAN
STARSTRIKE

In certain places in the Mortal Realms, the land is bombarded by fragments of magical ore that fall burning from the skies. These remnants of stars are coveted by ambitious warlords, as they can be used to forge deadly blades that will cut through any armour.

PITCHED BATTLE

Use the Pitched Battle rules from pages 72-75.

OBJECTIVES

3 objectives will be set up during the battle (see Starstrike).

SET-UP

The players alternate setting up units one at a time, starting with Player A. Players must set up units wholly within their own territory and more than 12" from enemy territory. The territories are shown on the map.

Continue to set up units until both players have set up their armies. If one player finishes first, the opposing player sets up the rest of the units in their army, one after another.

STARSTRIKE

As the battle rages on, the skies above are illuminated by the streaking trails of meteors crashing down to earth.

At the start of the second battle round, before determining who has the first turn, set up 1 objective on the border between the players' territories. At the start of the third battle round, before determining who has the first turn, set up 2 more objectives, 1 in each player's territory. Roll a D6 and refer to the map to determine where each objective will be set up.

BATTLE LENGTH

The battle lasts for 5 battle rounds (or until the amount of time allocated for the battle runs out).

GLORIOUS VICTORY

The player with the most victory points at the end of the battle wins a **major victory**.

If the players are tied on victory points at the end of the battle, each player checks to see how many of their Auxiliary Objectives they have completed. If one player has completed more Auxiliary Objectives than their opponent, they win a **minor victory**. If both players have completed the same number of Auxiliary Objectives, the battle is a **draw**.

VICTORY POINTS

Each player scores victory points at the end of each of their turns for each objective they control. The number of victory points is equal to the number of the current battle round. For example, a player who controls 1 objective at the end of their turn in the third battle round scores 3 victory points.

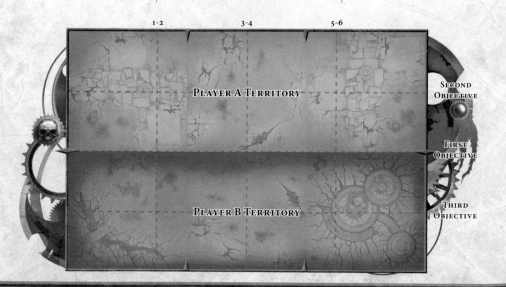

1-2   3-4   5-6

PLAYER A TERRITORY

SECOND OBJECTIVE

FIRST OBJECTIVE

PLAYER B TERRITORY

THIRD OBJECTIVE

BATTLEPLAN
SCORCHED EARTH

In war, it is often crucial to utterly destroy an enemy's ability to retaliate. Two armies have met on the border of their territories, each seeking to burn the precious resources of their foes to ash.

PITCHED BATTLE
Use the Pitched Battle rules from pages 72-75.

OBJECTIVES
Set up 8 objectives, 4 objectives in each player's territory, as shown on the map.

SET-UP
The players alternate setting up units one at a time, starting with Player A. Players must set up units wholly within their own territory and more than 9" from enemy territory. The territories are shown on the map.

Continue to set up units until both players have set up their armies. If one player finishes first, the opposing player sets up the rest of the units in their army, one after another.

BATTLE LENGTH
The battle lasts for 5 battle rounds (or until the amount of time allocated for the battle runs out).

GLORIOUS VICTORY
The player with the most victory points at the end of the battle wins a **major victory**.

If the players are tied on victory points at the end of the battle, each player checks to see how many of their Auxiliary Objectives they have completed. If one player has completed more Auxiliary Objectives than their opponent, they win a **minor victory**. If both players have completed the same number of Auxiliary Objectives, the battle is a **draw**.

VICTORY POINTS
At the end of each of their turns, each player scores 1 victory point for each objective they control.

Starting from the second battle round, at the end of each of their turns, a player can raze an objective they control in enemy territory. An objective in enemy territory cannot be razed while there is an enemy Leader unit within 6" of it.

If they do so, they score D3 victory points instead of 1, but the objective is removed from play.

If a player controls an objective in enemy territory while there is a friendly Leader unit within 6" of it, they score 1 additional victory point when it is razed.

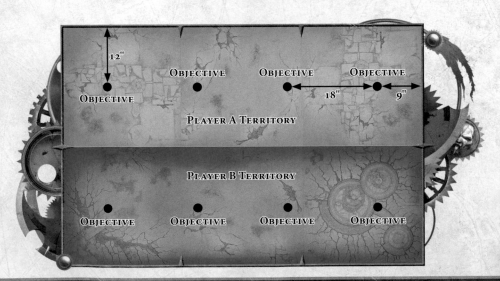

12"

OBJECTIVE　　OBJECTIVE　　OBJECTIVE

OBJECTIVE　　　　　　　18"　　　9"

PLAYER A TERRITORY

PLAYER B TERRITORY

OBJECTIVE　　OBJECTIVE　　OBJECTIVE　　OBJECTIVE

BATTLEPLAN
FOCAL POINTS

In this region, five focal points of geomantic energy are arranged in a square formation. Energy surges between these focal points, and it can be harnessed for use in rituals of awesome power.

PITCHED BATTLE
Use the Pitched Battle rules from pages 72-75.

OBJECTIVES
Set up 5 objectives, 1 objective in the centre of the battlefield and 2 objectives in each player's territory, as shown on the map.

SET-UP
The players alternate setting up units one at a time, starting with Player A. Players must set up units wholly within their own territory and more than 9" from enemy territory. The territories are shown on the map.

Continue to set up units until both players have set up their armies. If one player finishes first, the opposing player sets up the rest of the units in their army, one after another.

BATTLE LENGTH
The battle lasts for 5 battle rounds (or until the amount of time allocated for the battle runs out).

GLORIOUS VICTORY
The player with the most victory points at the end of the battle wins a **major victory**.

If the players are tied on victory points at the end of the battle, each player checks to see how many of their Auxiliary Objectives they have completed. If one player has completed more Auxiliary Objectives than their opponent, they win a **minor victory**. If both players have completed the same number of Auxiliary Objectives, the battle is a **draw**.

VICTORY POINTS
Each player scores victory points at the end of each of their turns as follows:

• If a player controls both objectives 1 and 3, they score 3 victory points.

• If a player controls both objectives 2 and 4, they score 3 victory points.

• If a player controls the central objective, they score 2 victory points.

• If a player controls any other objective, they score 1 victory point for each objective.

• If a player controls an objective while there is a friendly **Monster** or friendly Behemoth unit within 6" of it, they score 1 additional victory point.

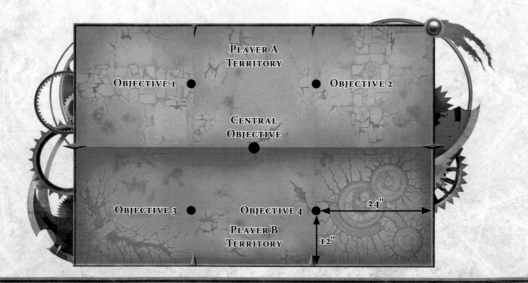

BATTLEPLAN
THE BETTER PART OF VALOUR

It is important to learn when to hold on in order to ensure victory and when to fall back in the face of unbeatable odds. A battle can be decided by the general who is most capable of resolving this difficult dilemma.

PITCHED BATTLE
Use the Pitched Battle rules from pages 72-75.

OBJECTIVES
Set up 6 objectives as shown on the map.

SET-UP
The players alternate setting up units one at a time, starting with Player A. Players must set up units wholly within their own territory and more than 9" from enemy territory. The territories are shown on the map.

Continue to set up units until both players have set up their armies. If one player finishes first, the opposing player sets up the rest of the units in their army, one after another.

CONTEST OF STRENGTH
Sometimes, victory rests in the hands of the seemingly meekest of warriors.

The normal rules for controlling an objective are not used in this battle. Instead, a player controls an objective if a friendly Battleline unit finishes a move within 3" of the objective, unless that move was a retreat move. The player loses control of that objective if the Battleline unit is not within 3" of it or is destroyed. Only 1 Battleline unit can control each objective at a time – if more than 1 unit is eligible, then the first to arrive controls it. If an enemy unit controlling an objective is destroyed by an attack made with a melee weapon by a Battleline unit, then the attacking unit immediately gains control of that objective, as long as they are within 3" of it.

BATTLE LENGTH
The battle lasts for 5 battle rounds (or until the amount of time allocated for the battle runs out).

GLORIOUS VICTORY
The player with the most victory points at the end of the battle wins a **major victory**. If the players are tied on victory points at the end of the battle, each player checks to see how many of their Auxiliary Objectives they have completed. If one player has completed more Auxiliary Objectives than their opponent, they win a **minor victory**. If both players

have completed the same number of Auxiliary Objectives, the battle is a **draw**.

VICTORY POINTS
Starting from the second battle round, at the end of each of their turns, a player can destroy 1 or more of the objectives they control in order to score the following victory points:

- If the player gained control of the objective in this turn, they score 1 victory point.

- If the player controlled the objective at the end of their last turn and has not lost control of it since, they score 2 victory points.

- If the player controlled the objective at the end of their turn before last and has not lost control of it since, they score 4 victory points.

- If the player gained control of the objective in the first battle round and has not lost control of it by the end of their turn in the fifth battle round, they score 8 victory points.

If more than one of these criteria applies, use the one that scores the most victory points. Once destroyed, an objective is removed from play.

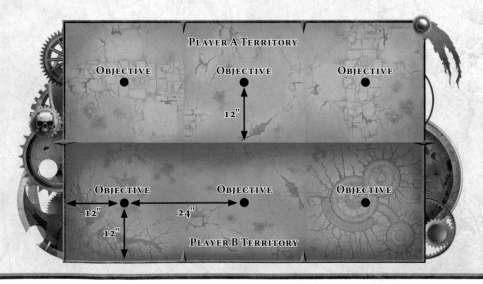

BATTLEPLAN
SHIFTING OBJECTIVES

In order to be successful, a general must learn to react with lightning swiftness to the changing conditions of battle, striking with all their might first in one direction and then in another in order to ensure victory.

PITCHED BATTLE
Use the Pitched Battle rules from pages 72-75.

OBJECTIVES
Set up 3 objectives along the centre of the battlefield, as shown on the map.

SET-UP
The players alternate setting up units one at a time, starting with Player A. Players must set up units wholly within their own territory. The territories are shown on the map.

Continue to set up units until both players have set up their armies. If one player finishes first, the opposing player sets up the rest of the units in their army, one after another.

PRIMARY AND SECONDARY OBJECTIVES
As the battle rages on, certain areas of ground can suddenly become more – or less – valuable to the army that controls them.

At the start of each battle round, before determining who has the first turn, roll a D3. The objective with the corresponding number is the primary objective for that battle round, and the other 2 objectives are the secondary objectives for that battle round.

BATTLE LENGTH
The battle lasts for 5 battle rounds (or until the amount of time allocated for the battle runs out).

GLORIOUS VICTORY
The player with the most victory points at the end of the battle wins a **major victory**.

If the players are tied on victory points at the end of the battle, each player checks to see how many of their Auxiliary Objectives they have completed. If one player has completed more Auxiliary Objectives than their opponent, they win a **minor victory**. If both players have completed the same number of Auxiliary Objectives, the battle is a **draw**.

VICTORY POINTS
Each player scores victory points at the end of each of their turns as follows:

- If the player controls the primary objective, they score 2 victory points.

- For each secondary objective the player controls, they score 1 victory point.

- If a player controls an objective while there is a friendly Battleline unit within 6" of it, they score 1 additional victory point.

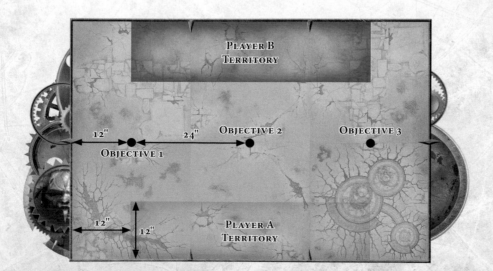

BATTLEPLAN
PLACES OF ARCANE POWER

2020

The leaders of two rival armies have learnt the location of three places of arcane power. If a mighty warrior stands upon such a location, they can leech some of the arcane energy stored within.

PITCHED BATTLE
Use the Pitched Battle rules from pages 72-75.

OBJECTIVES
Set up 3 objectives as shown on the map.

SET-UP
The players alternate setting up units one at a time, starting with Player A. Players must set up units wholly within their own territory and more than 9" from enemy territory. The territories are shown on the map.

Continue to set up units until both players have set up their armies. If one player finishes first, the opposing player sets up the rest of the units in their army, one after another.

HEROIC CONQUEST
Now is the time for great champions and mighty warlords to prove their worth and take what is theirs.

The normal rules for controlling an objective are not used in this battle. Instead, a player controls an objective if a Leader unit from their army finishes a move within 3" of the objective, unless that move was a retreat move. The player loses control of that objective if that Leader unit is not within 3" of it or is destroyed.

Only 1 Leader unit can control each objective at a time – if more than 1 unit is eligible, then the first to arrive controls it. If an enemy unit controlling an objective is destroyed by an attack made with a melee weapon by a Leader unit, then the attacking unit immediately gains control of that objective, as long as they are within 3" of it.

BATTLE LENGTH
The battle lasts for 5 battle rounds (or until the amount of time allocated for the battle runs out).

GLORIOUS VICTORY
The player with the most victory points at the end of the battle wins a **major victory**.

If the players are tied on victory points at the end of the battle, each player checks to see how many of their Auxiliary Objectives they have completed. If one player has completed more Auxiliary Objectives than their opponent, they win a **minor victory**. If both players have completed the same number of Auxiliary Objectives, the battle is a **draw**.

VICTORY POINTS
Each player scores victory points at the end of each of their turns for each objective they control. The number of victory points is equal to the number of consecutive turns the player has controlled the objective for: 1 victory point on the turn they gained control, 2 victory points at the end of their second turn, and so on.

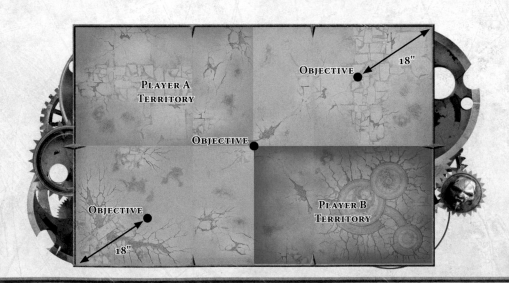

BATTLEPLAN
THE BLADE'S EDGE

Two armies collide on sacred ground that is prized by both generals. So close are the key areas of control that rival warriors cannot help but come into contact, no matter where they choose to make their stand.

PITCHED BATTLE

Use the Pitched Battle rules from pages 72-75.

OBJECTIVES

Set up 6 objectives, 3 objectives in each player's territory, as shown on the map.

At the start of each battle round after the first, the player taking the second turn in that battle round can pick 1 objective on the battlefield and remove it from play.

SET-UP

The players alternate setting up units one at a time, starting with Player A. Players must set up units wholly within their own territory and more than 12" from enemy territory. The territories are shown on the map.

Continue to set up units until both players have set up their armies. If one player finishes first, the opposing player sets up the rest of the units in their army, one after another.

BATTLE LENGTH

The battle lasts for 5 battle rounds (or until the amount of time allocated for the battle runs out).

GLORIOUS VICTORY

The player with the most victory points at the end of the battle wins a **major victory**.

If the players are tied on victory points at the end of the battle, each player checks to see how many of their Auxiliary Objectives they have completed. If one player has completed more Auxiliary Objectives than their opponent, they win a **minor victory**. If both players have completed the same number of Auxiliary Objectives, the battle is a **draw**.

VICTORY POINTS

Each player scores 1 victory point at the end of each of their turns for each objective they control.

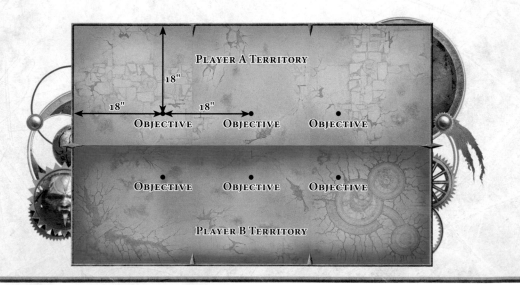

PLAYER A TERRITORY

18"

18"   18"

OBJECTIVE   OBJECTIVE   OBJECTIVE

OBJECTIVE   OBJECTIVE   OBJECTIVE

PLAYER B TERRITORY

BATTLEPLAN
TOTAL COMMITMENT

A battle has been raging for days between two equally matched opponents. Both armies are committed to the fight, and neither side has any reserves left to draw upon.

PITCHED BATTLE
Use the Pitched Battle rules from pages 72-75.

OBJECTIVES
Set up 4 objectives, 2 objectives in each player's territory, as shown on the map.

SET-UP
The players alternate setting up units one at a time, starting with Player A. Players must set up units wholly within their own territory and more than 9" from enemy territory. The territories are shown on the map.

Continue to set up units until both players have set up their armies. If one player finishes first, the opposing player sets up the rest of the units in their army, one after another.

NO RESERVES
In this battle, all units must be set up on the battlefield before the battle begins. Any unit that is set up as a reserve is destroyed and all of the models in the unit are slain.

BATTLE LENGTH
The battle lasts for 5 battle rounds (or until the amount of time allocated for the battle runs out).

GLORIOUS VICTORY
The player with the most victory points at the end of the battle wins a **major victory**.

If the players are tied on victory points at the end of the battle, each player checks to see how many of their Auxiliary Objectives they have completed. If one player has completed more Auxiliary Objectives than their opponent, they win a **minor victory**. If both players have completed the same number of Auxiliary Objectives, the battle is a **draw**.

VICTORY POINTS
Each player scores victory points at the end of each of their turns as follows:

• For each objective the player controls in their own territory, they score 1 victory point.

• For each objective the player controls in their opponent's territory, they score 3 victory points.

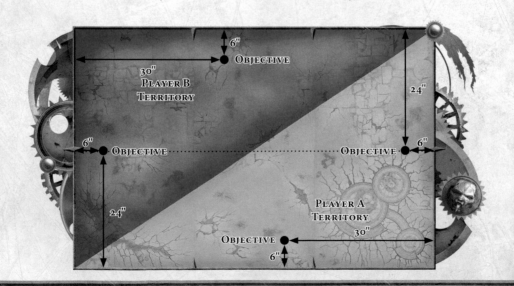

BATTLEPLAN
FORCING THE HAND

A long-running stalemate has brought two opposing armies to the edge of contested territory. Both generals must now strive to lure their rival into making a costly mistake, if they wish to break this grinding deadlock in a decisive fashion.

PITCHED BATTLE
Use the Pitched Battle rules from pages 72-75.

OBJECTIVES
Set up 6 objectives, 3 objectives in each player's territory, as shown on the map.

SET-UP
The players alternate setting up units one at a time, starting with Player A. Players must set up units wholly within their own territory and more than 12" from enemy territory. The territories are shown on the map.

Continue to set up units until both players have set up their armies. If one player finishes first, the opposing player sets up the rest of the units in their army, one after another.

PRIMARY OBJECTIVE
Both sides are attempting to hold on to their own coveted ground, even as they strive to oust their foes from the land.

The map shows which objectives belong to which player. At the start of each player's turn, the opposing player picks 1 of their own objectives to be the primary objective for that turn. For example, if it is Player A's turn, Player B picks one of the Player B objectives labelled on the map to be the primary objective that turn.

BATTLE LENGTH
The battle lasts for 5 battle rounds (or until the amount of time allocated for the battle runs out).

GLORIOUS VICTORY
The player with the most victory points at the end of the battle wins a **major victory**.

If the players are tied on victory points at the end of the battle, each player checks to see how many of their Auxiliary Objectives they have completed. If one player has completed more Auxiliary Objectives than their opponent, they win a **minor victory**. If both players have completed the same number of Auxiliary Objectives, the battle is a **draw**.

VICTORY POINTS
Each player scores victory points at the end of each of their turns as follows:

- If a player controls the primary objective, they score 3 victory points.

- If the player controls any other objective, they score 1 victory point for each objective.

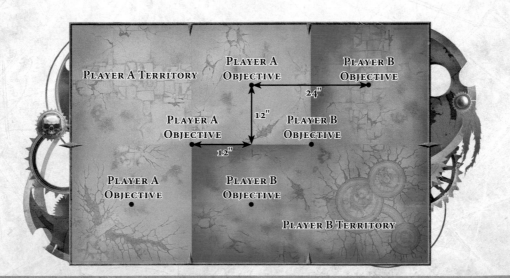

PLAYER A TERRITORY

PLAYER A OBJECTIVE

PLAYER B OBJECTIVE

24"

PLAYER A OBJECTIVE

12"

PLAYER B OBJECTIVE

12"

PLAYER A OBJECTIVE

PLAYER B OBJECTIVE

PLAYER B TERRITORY

MEETING ENGAGEMENTS (2020)

The following rules allow you to play Meeting Engagements, games that are designed to allow players to fight a battle on a small-sized battlefield in less than 90 minutes. These rules are ideal for games where the players have a limited amount of space or time and for one-day tournaments.

The Meeting Engagement rules are designed to allow players to play a matched play game with a 1,000-point army on a battlefield no larger than a typical dining table. What's more, Meeting Engagements are quick, allowing you to play two games in almost the same amount of time as a single Pitched Battle or complete a five-round tournament in a single day.

However, you will quickly discover that just because a Meeting Engagement can be played quickly does not mean it is any less of a challenge than a regular Pitched Battle!

MEETING ENGAGEMENT CHART			
	Spearhead	Main Body	Rearguard
Leader	0-1	1-2	0-1
Behemoth	0	0-1	0-1
Artillery	0	0	0-2
Battleline	0-1	1+	0-2
Other units	0-2	0+	0-2
Double-sized units	None	Battleline	Any
Unit limits	Up to 2 units per warscroll		

SPECIAL RULE

The following rule applies to all matched play games:

You cannot make more than 1 dice roll (excluding re-rolls) to negate a wound or mortal wound that has been allocated to a model. If you could use more than one ability to negate allocated wounds or mortal wounds, you must pick which ability you will use.

PICKING YOUR ARMY

To play a Meeting Engagement, you and your opponent will first need to pick your armies. Meeting Engagements use Pitched Battle profiles to determine a unit's minimum and maximum size and points cost. These profiles can be found in the *Pitched Battle Profiles 2020* book or in the battletome where the warscroll for the unit appears. The following restrictions apply when picking your army:

ALLEGIANCE

In a Meeting Engagement, you must pick an allegiance for your army as described in the core rules. All of the units in the army must either have that allegiance or be allied to that allegiance (see below).

POINTS LIMIT

You can spend up to 1,000 points on the units in your army.

WARSCROLL BATTALIONS

Your army can include up to 1 warscroll battalion. Note that you must pay the cost of the units in the battalion normally – the points value listed for each battalion is an extra cost that allows you to use it.

UNIT LIMITS

Your army cannot include more than 2 units chosen from the same warscroll, unless those units are part of a warscroll battalion in your army.

CONTINGENTS

You must split your army into a spearhead contingent, main body contingent and rearguard contingent. Each contingent must have at least 1 unit and conform to the restrictions on the Meeting Engagement chart above.

UNIT SIZES

Your army cannot include units that are larger than their minimum unit size unless they are main body Battleline units or rearguard units. Main body Battleline units and rearguard units can be up to double their minimum unit size.

ALLIES

Your army can include up to 1 allied unit. It cannot be larger than its minimum unit size. It is not included when working out the number of Battleline units in the army but does count towards the number of Leaders, Behemoths and Artillery units.

ENDLESS SPELLS

By paying an endless spell's points cost, all **Wizards** in your army know that endless spell, and you can use (and re-use) 1 endless spell model of the appropriate type in the battle. You can only pay the points for 1 endless spell in a Meeting Engagement.

COMMAND POINTS

You can purchase up to 1 extra command point for 50 points. Add the extra command point to the command points you receive at the start of the battle.

TERRAIN: PRIMARY LIST	TERRAIN: SECONDARY LIST
Azyrite Ruin	Azyrite Ruin
Baleful Realmgate	Baleful Realmgate
Numinous Occulum	Ophidian Archway
Shattered Temple (single terrain feature that counts as both your primary and secondary terrain)	Timeworn Ruins (consisting of 3 models instead of 10)
Sigmarite Dais (single terrain feature that counts as both your primary and secondary terrain)	Warcry Statue Head
Wyldwood	Warcry Belltower
Unique: Any other terrain feature no more than 10" across and 18" tall	**Unique:** Any other terrain feature no more than 6" across and 6" tall

ARMY ROSTER

Once you have picked your army, record the details on a piece of paper (your army roster) and show it to your opponent before setting up your army at the start of the battle.

The roster must include a list of the units in each contingent; the warscroll battalion, allied unit and endless spell (if any) included in your army; what size the units are; the army's allegiance; if you have purchased an extra command point; and which model is the army's general.

Use the notes column for each unit to record any command models you have chosen for it, the spells that are known by the **Wizards** in your army, any artefacts or other items wielded by **Heroes** in your army, and which command trait you have chosen for your general.

In a Meeting Engagement, your general must be a Leader and cannot be an ally. If your general is slain in a Meeting Engagement, do not pick a new one.

If your army includes any units that are given keywords when they are set up, such as units with a Mark of Chaos, these must be written down when the unit is added to the roster.

An example Meeting Engagement roster can be found in this book (pg 129).

MEETING ENGAGEMENT BATTLEPLANS

We have provided 6 battleplans designed for use in Meeting Engagements. Before setting up the battlefield, pick a battleplan by rolling a dice and consulting the table below.

D6 Battleplan

1   The Centre Ground (pg 92)
2   Death Pass (pg 93)
3   The Borderline (pg 94)
4   The Raid (pg 95)
5   Caught Off Guard (pg 96)
6   Changing Priorities (pg 97)

AUXILIARY OBJECTIVES

In a Meeting Engagement, Auxiliary Objectives are used as described on pages 108-109. In addition, if an Auxiliary Objective requires you to pick a unit in a player's starting army, you can pick a unit from any of the contingents in that army instead of a unit that was set up before the first battle round.

BATTLEFIELDS

A Meeting Engagement is fought on a battlefield that measures 30-36" by 40-48". After generating the battleplan that will be used, the players must first set up the objective markers and then the terrain features for the battle on the battlefield. The players can then proceed to set up their armies.

The location of any objectives can be found on the battleplan that is

being used. After the objectives have been set up, each player must pick 2 terrain features from the lists to the left – 1 from the primary list and 1 from the secondary list.

The players then roll off and alternate setting up their terrain features, one at a time, starting with the player who won the roll-off. Terrain features must be set up more than 3" from the edge of the battlefield, more than 3" from any other terrain features and more than 1" from any objectives. Sometimes this will make it impossible for a terrain feature to be set up; in this case, it is not used.

After the players have set up the terrain features for the battle, they can proceed to set up their armies, as described on pages 90-91 and in the battleplan they are using.

FACTION TERRAIN

Sometimes the allegiance abilities for an army will allow it to include 1 or more terrain features, or a warscroll will allow you to set up 1 or more terrain features once the battle has begun. These are set up in addition to the terrain features that have been set up as previously described.

In a Meeting Engagement, faction terrain must be set up more than 3" from any other terrain features and more than 1" from any objectives, in addition to any other restrictions that apply. Sometimes this will make it impossible for a faction terrain piece to be set up; in this case, it is not used.

SCENERY RULES

In a Meeting Engagement, you must randomly generate a scenery rule from the Scenery table in the core rules for each unique terrain feature. A terrain feature is **unique** if it is not included in the terrain lists above, even if it has a warscroll.

TRIUMPHS

In a Meeting Engagement, do not roll on the Triumph table in the core rules if you won your last battle. Instead, the player who spent fewer points when selecting their army can roll on the Triumph table in the Pitched Battle section on page 75.

MEETING ENGAGEMENT SET-UP

In a Meeting Engagement, one contingent from each player's army is set up on the battlefield before the start of the battle, and the remaining contingents are set up on the battlefield during the battle. The battleplan being used will explain when each contingent must be set up.

ARRIVAL TIME

Each contingent has an arrival time, which is when it must be set up on the battlefield. This will be indicated on the map included in the battleplan and will specify either 'Start', 'Turn 1' or 'Turn 2'. Contingents with the 'Start' arrival time are set up before the start of the battle, contingents with the 'Turn 1' arrival time are set up at the end of the controlling player's first turn, and contingents with the 'Turn 2' arrival time are set up at the end of the controlling player's second turn. Any units that cannot be set up at their contingent's arrival time for any reason are destroyed.

ARRIVAL EDGE

Each contingent has an arrival edge, which is indicated on the

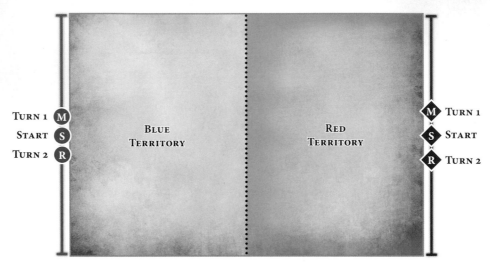

Each spearhead contingent (S) is set up before the start of the battle. The main body contingents (M) are set up at the end of the controlling player's first turn, and the rearguard contingents (R) are set up at the end of the controlling player's second turn. All three contingents in each army have the same arrival edge and must be set up wholly within 3" of it.

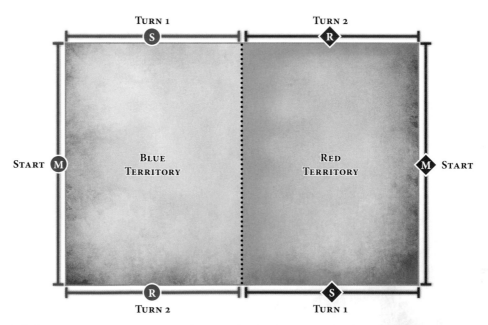

Each main body contingent (M) is set up before the start of the battle. The spearhead contingents (S) are set up at the end of the controlling player's first turn, and the rearguard contingents (R) are set up at the end of the controlling player's second turn. Each contingent has a different arrival edge and must be set up wholly within 3" of that edge.

map included in the battleplan. When a contingent is set up on the battlefield, set up all of the units in that contingent wholly within 3" of that contingent's arrival edge.

Two example maps are shown on the left. The thick coloured lines beside the battlefield edges indicate the contingents' arrival edges, while the labels for each contingent indicate that contingent's arrival time.

RESERVE UNITS

In a Meeting Engagement, reserve units cannot be set up on the battlefield before the arrival time of the contingent to which those units belong. If a reserve unit has to be set up on the battlefield at a specific point – e.g. at the start of the controlling player's first turn – but that point comes before the contingent's arrival time, that unit cannot be used as a reserve unit in that battle: either set that unit up with the rest of its contingent or do not use that unit.

Reserve units otherwise follow the normal set-up rules for such a unit (they do not have to be set up wholly within 3" of an arrival edge).

NEW UNITS

Any new unit you add to your army during the battle – e.g. units that can be summoned – are not considered to be part of any contingent. Follow the normal set-up rules for that unit (they do not have to be set up wholly within 3" of an arrival edge).

OVERFLOW

Sometimes you will not be able to fit a model or unit wholly within 3" of its arrival edge. When this is the case, set up the model or unit so that it overlaps the arrival edge, making sure that as much of the model's base or the unit's bases are on the battlefield as possible. A model or unit cannot be set up with its base(s) overlapping an edge other than its arrival edge.

DEADLY TERRITORY

When reserve or new units are set up on the battlefield during a Meeting Engagement, they must treat enemy arrival edges in the same way as an enemy model. Usually this will mean that they cannot be set up within 9" of an enemy arrival edge.

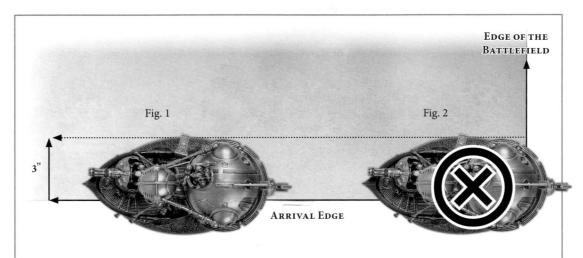

EDGE OF THE BATTLEFIELD

Fig. 1   Fig. 2

3"

ARRIVAL EDGE

This model cannot fit within 3" of its arrival edge, and so it can be set up as shown in Fig. 1, with its base overlapping its arrival edge. It cannot be set up as shown in Fig. 2, because its base is overlapping an edge of the battlefield that is not its arrival edge.

BATTLEPLAN
THE CENTRE GROUND

Two armies converge, each one determined to control the battlefield by holding the centre ground. A brutal conflict erupts as each army surges forwards to control the vital location.

MEETING ENGAGEMENT

Use the Meeting Engagement rules from pages 88-91.

OBJECTIVES

Set up 2 objectives on the border between the players' territories, as shown on the map.

SET-UP

The players roll off, and the winner decides who will command the red army and who will command the blue army.

The players then alternate setting up units from their spearhead contingent one at a time, starting with the player who won the roll-off.

Continue to set up units until both players have set up their spearhead contingents. The remaining contingents will arrive during the battle as indicated on the map.

BATTLE LENGTH

The battle lasts for 4 battle rounds.

GLORIOUS VICTORY

At the end of the battle, if one player has 1-4 more victory points than their opponent, they win a **minor victory**. If one player has 5 or more victory points than their opponent, they win a **major victory**.

If the players are tied on victory points at the end of the battle, each player checks to see how many of their Auxiliary Objectives they have completed. If one player has completed more Auxiliary Objectives than their opponent, they win a **minor victory**. If both players have completed the same number of Auxiliary Objectives, the battle is a **draw**.

VICTORY POINTS

Victory points are scored as follows:

• At the end of each battle round, each player adds up the Wounds characteristics of all enemy models that were slain during that battle round. The player with the higher total scores 2 victory points. If neither player has a higher total, each player scores 1 victory point.

• At the end of each battle round, the player who controls the most objectives scores 3 victory points. If both players control an equal number of objectives, each player scores 1 victory point.

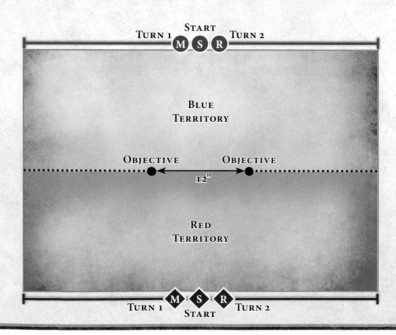

START
TURN 1 M S R TURN 2

BLUE TERRITORY

OBJECTIVE ←————→ OBJECTIVE
12"

RED TERRITORY

M S R
TURN 1 **START** TURN 2

BATTLEPLAN
DEATH PASS

Two armies clash head-on in a pass that is the only way through a mountain range. With each side determined to control this vital ingress, a brutal conflict erupts as they surge forwards to drive off the foe.

MEETING ENGAGEMENT
Use the Meeting Engagement rules from pages 88-91.

OBJECTIVES
Set up 4 objectives, 1 objective in the centre of each territory and 2 objectives on the border between the players' territories, as shown on the map.

SET-UP
The players roll off, and the winner decides who will command the red army and who will command the blue army.

The players then alternate setting up units from their spearhead contingent onc at a time, starting with the player who won the roll-off.

Continue to set up units until both players have set up their spearhead contingents. The remaining contingents will arrive during the battle as indicated on the map.

BATTLE LENGTH
The battle lasts for 4 battle rounds.

GLORIOUS VICTORY
At the end of the battle, if one player has 1-4 more victory points than their opponent, they win a **minor victory**. If one player has 5 or more victory points than their opponent, they win a **major victory**.

If the players are tied on victory points at the end of the battle, each player checks to see how many of their Auxiliary Objectives they have completed. If one player has completed more Auxiliary Objectives than their opponent, they win a **minor victory**. If both players have completed the same number of Auxiliary Objectives, the battle is a **draw**.

VICTORY POINTS
Victory points are scored as follows:

• At the end of each battle round, each player adds up the Wounds characteristics of all enemy models that were slain during that battle round. The player with the higher total scores 2 victory points. If neither player has a higher total, each player scores 1 victory point.

• At the end of each battle round, the player who controls the most objectives scores 3 victory points. If both players control an equal number of objectives, each player scores 1 victory point.

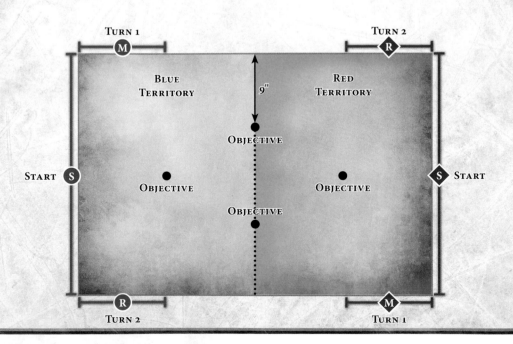

BATTLEPLAN
THE BORDERLINE

A border between two territories is constantly being fought over. Neither side will allow the enemy to occupy the border without blood being shed.

MEETING ENGAGEMENT
Use the Meeting Engagement rules from pages 88-91.

OBJECTIVES
Set up 3 objectives, 1 objective in the centre of the battlefield and 2 objectives on the border between the players' territories, as shown on the map.

SET-UP
The players roll off, and the winner decides who will command the red army and who will command the blue army.

The players then alternate setting up units from their spearhead contingent one at a time, starting with the player who won the roll-off.

Continue to set up units until both players have set up their spearhead contingents. The remaining contingents will arrive during the battle as indicated on the map.

BATTLE LENGTH
The battle lasts for 4 battle rounds.

GLORIOUS VICTORY
At the end of the battle, if one player has 1-4 more victory points than their opponent, they win a **minor victory**. If one player has 5 or more victory points than their opponent, they win a **major victory**.

If the players are tied on victory points at the end of the battle, each player checks to see how many of their Auxiliary Objectives they have completed. If one player has completed more Auxiliary Objectives than their opponent, they win a **minor victory**. If both players have completed the same number of Auxiliary Objectives, the battle is a **draw**.

VICTORY POINTS
Victory points are scored as follows:

- At the end of each battle round, each player adds up the Wounds characteristics of all enemy models that were slain during that battle round. The player with the higher total scores 2 victory points. If neither player has a higher total, each player scores 1 victory point.

- At the end of each battle round, the player who controls the most objectives scores 3 victory points. If both players control an equal number of objectives, each player scores 1 victory point.

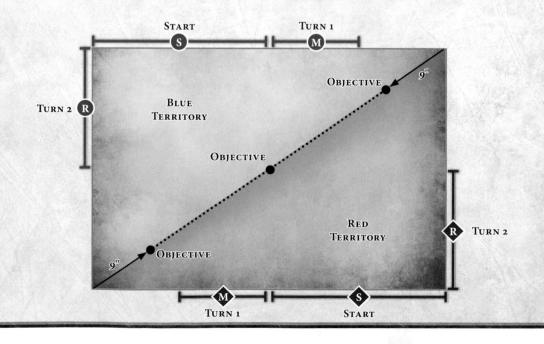

BATTLEPLAN
THE RAID

Sometimes battles are fought not to destroy the enemy but to seize their resources and carry them off. Raiding parties will strike into enemy territory, capturing an objective and searching for any hidden treasures, before razing what remains to the ground to deny its use to the enemy.

MEETING ENGAGEMENT
Use the Meeting Engagement rules from pages 88-91.

OBJECTIVES
Set up 4 objectives, 1 objective in the centre of each quarter of the battlefield, as shown on the map.

SET-UP
The players roll off, and the winner decides who will command the red army and who will command the blue army.

The players then alternate setting up units from their spearhead contingent one at a time, starting with the player who won the roll-off.

Continue to set up units until both players have set up their spearhead contingents. The remaining contingents will arrive during the battle as indicated on the map.

Note that in this battle, units from each player's rearguard can arrive by one or both of the narrow edges of the battlefield.

BATTLE LENGTH
The battle lasts for 4 battle rounds.

GLORIOUS VICTORY
At the end of the battle, if one player has 1-4 more victory points than their opponent, they win a **minor victory**. If one player has 5 or more victory points than their opponent, they win a **major victory**.

If the players are tied on victory points at the end of the battle, each player checks to see how many of their Auxiliary Objectives they have completed. If one player has completed more Auxiliary Objectives than their opponent, they win a **minor victory**. If both players

have completed the same number of Auxiliary Objectives, the battle is a **draw**.

VICTORY POINTS
Victory points are scored as follows:

- At the end of each battle round, each player adds up the Wounds characteristics of all enemy models that were slain during that battle round. The player with the higher total scores 2 victory points. If neither player has a higher total, each player scores 1 victory point.

- At the end of each battle round, the player who controls the most objectives scores 3 victory points. If both players control an equal number of objectives, each player scores 1 victory point.

- Starting from the second battle round, at the start of their hero phase, a player can raze an objective they control in enemy territory. If they do so, they score D3 victory points, but the objective is removed from play.

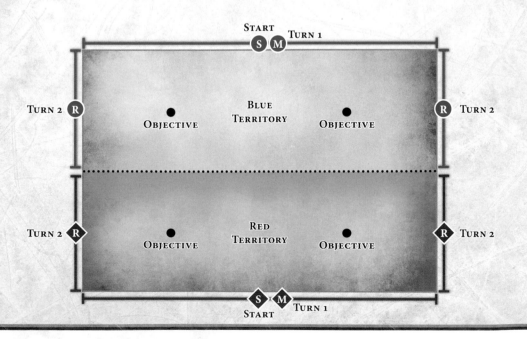

BATTLEPLAN
CAUGHT OFF GUARD

One army approaches its opponent from behind, aiming to take their enemy by surprise.

MEETING ENGAGEMENT

Use the Meeting Engagement rules from pages 88-91.

OBJECTIVES

Set up 3 objectives, 1 objective in the centre of the battlefield and 1 objective in the centre of each player's territory, as shown on the map.

SET-UP

The players roll off. The winner will command the red army for this battle and their opponent will command the blue army.

The player in command of the blue army then picks either their main body or rearguard contingent to start the battle. The contingent that they did not pick will arrive at the end of Turn 2. Their spearhead contingent will arrive at the end of Turn 1.

The players then alternate setting up units one at a time, starting with the player who won the roll-off. The player in command of the red army sets up units from their spearhead contingent, and the player in command of the blue army sets up units from their chosen contingent.

Continue to set up units until both players have set up their starting contingents. The remaining contingents will arrive during the battle as indicated on the map.

BATTLE LENGTH

The battle lasts for 4 battle rounds.

GLORIOUS VICTORY

At the end of the battle, if one player has 1-4 more victory points than their opponent, they win a **minor victory.** If one player has 5 or more victory points than their opponent, they win a **major victory**.

If the players are tied on victory points at the end of the battle, each player checks to see how many of their Auxiliary Objectives they have completed. If one player has completed more Auxiliary Objectives than their opponent, they win a **minor victory**. If both players have completed the same number of Auxiliary Objectives, the battle is a **draw**.

VICTORY POINTS

Victory points are scored as follows:

• At the end of each battle round, each player adds up the Wounds characteristics of all enemy models that were slain during that battle round. The player with the higher total scores 2 victory points. If neither player has a higher total, each player scores 1 victory point.

• At the end of each battle round, the player who controls the most objectives scores 3 victory points. If both players control an equal number of objectives, each player scores 1 victory point.

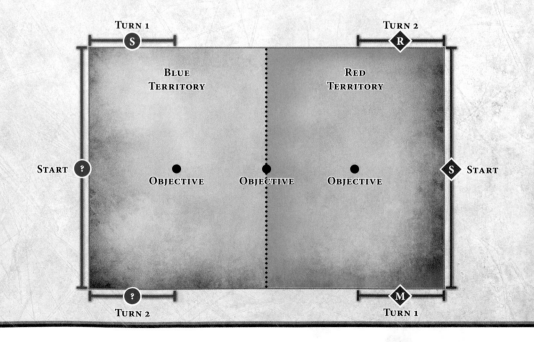

BATTLEPLAN
CHANGING PRIORITIES

Sometimes during battle, the objectives that will determine the winner will change from moment to moment. The victor will be the general who is best able to modify their plans to suit the changing conditions.

MEETING ENGAGEMENT
Use the Meeting Engagement rules from pages 88-91.

OBJECTIVES
Set up 3 objectives along the border between the players' territories, as shown on the map.

SET-UP
The players roll off, and the winner decides who will command the red army and who will command the blue army.

The players then alternate setting up units from their spearhead contingent one at a time, starting with the player who won the roll-off.

Continue to set up units until both players have set up their spearhead

contingents. The remaining contingents will arrive during the battle as indicated on the map.

THE PRIORITIES
Great commanders must react decisively to changing circumstances.

At the start of each battle round, before determining which player has the first turn, the player in command of the red army must roll a dice. On a 1-2, objective 1 is the primary objective; on a 3-4, objective 2 is the primary objective; and on a 5-6, objective 3 is the primary objective.

BATTLE LENGTH
The battle lasts for 4 battle rounds.

GLORIOUS VICTORY
At the end of the battle, if one player has 1-4 more victory points than their opponent, they win a **minor victory**. If one player has 5 or more victory points than their opponent, they win a **major victory**.

If the players are tied on victory points at the end of the battle, each

player checks to see how many of their Auxiliary Objectives they have completed. If one player has completed more Auxiliary Objectives than their opponent, they win a **minor victory**. If both players have completed the same number of Auxiliary Objectives, the battle is a **draw**.

VICTORY POINTS
Victory points are scored as follows:

- At the end of each battle round, each player adds up the Wounds characteristics of all enemy models that were slain during that battle round. The player with the higher total scores 2 victory points. If neither player has a higher total, each player scores 1 victory point.

- At the end of each battle round, the player who controls the primary objective scores 3 victory points. If neither player controls the primary objective, the player who controls the most objectives scores 2 victory points. If neither player controls the primary objective and both players control an equal number of objectives, each player scores 1 victory point.

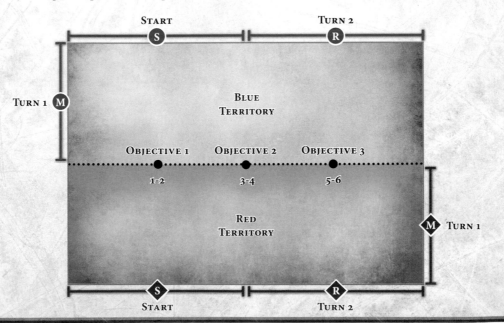

PITCHED BATTLE COALITION OF DEATH

This type of Pitched Battle allows you to play alongside a teammate in a 2v2 doubles format, where your allegiances weigh heavily on the effectiveness of your coalition. These rules can be used for one-off games or as part of a tournament.

To play a Pitched Battle Coalition of Death game, you must have 4 players split into two coalitions using any method preferred.

THE ARMIES

Each player must follow the Vanguard Pitched Battle chart restrictions (pg 72) when picking their armies.

Points, warscroll battalions and Battleline units in each individual army cannot be shared with another player's army in your coalition.

Each player commands the models in their army and is allowed to decide what they do, how they move, and so on, and that player makes all of the dice rolls for their own units. In addition, each player accrues their own command points and can use any allegiance abilities available to them as normal.

Models in other players' armies that are part of your coalition are considered to be neither friendly nor enemy models. This means that abilities used by your army that only affect friendly models or that only affect enemy models will not affect models from the other armies in your coalition.

Use the Pitched Battle rules on pages 72-75 for Pitched Battle Coalition of Death games except where modified below:

- Each player in a coalition must pick a faction allegiance (this cannot be a Grand Alliance).

- The same faction allegiance cannot be picked more than once in a coalition.

- A Unique unit cannot be included more than once in a coalition.

ALLIED UNITS

Different allegiances within an individual player's army must be able to ally following the normal rules.

GENERALS AND WARLORDS

Each player picks a general for their army as normal. You must also pick 1 player from each coalition to be the warlord.

If, at any time during the game, the coalition cannot decide in what order to carry out actions, the warlord has the final say on the order of events. In addition, if a dice needs to be rolled for the whole coalition, the warlord makes that dice roll. Finally, any victory conditions from a battleplan that apply to an army general only apply to the warlord's general, unless specifically noted otherwise.

THE COALITION

The individual armies that can create a coalition can be found on the Coalition Matrix (pg 100-101).

The following restrictions apply to these coalitions during Pitched Battle Coalition of Death games:

BATTLE-FORGED COALITION
- No restrictions.

FRACTIOUS COALITION
- At the start of your hero phase in the first battle round, you do not receive 1 command point.

DESPERATE COALITION
- At the start of your hero phase in the first battle round, you do not receive 1 command point.

- When making normal moves, you must treat units in other players' armies that are part of your coalition as enemy units.

COALITION OF DEATH RESTRICTIONS

These restrictions also apply to Pitched Battle Coalition of Death games.

ENDLESS SPELLS

If one player in a coalition has spent the points for an endless spell, only **Wizards** in that player's army know and may use that endless spell, providing that they are able to cast it.

BATTLEPLANS

Use the Pitched Battle Battleplans on pages 76-87 for a Pitched Battle Coalition of Death game.

AUXILIARY OBJECTIVES

In a Pitched Battle Coalition of Death game, Auxiliary Objectives are used as described on pages 108-109 in addition to the following restrictions:

- Each individual player in a coalition picks 1 Auxiliary Objective instead of 2.

- The same Auxiliary Objective cannot be picked more than once by the same coalition.

SPECIAL RULE

The following rule applies to all matched play games:

You cannot make more than 1 dice roll (excluding re-rolls) to negate a wound or mortal wound that has been allocated to a model. If you could use more than one ability to negate allocated wounds or mortal wounds, you must pick which ability you will use.

COALITION OF DEATH SPECIAL RULES

The following special rules apply to all Pitched Battle Coalition of Death games:

- Any reference to 'the player' or 'the players' is instead treated as 'the coalition' or 'the coalitions'.

- Any objectives that are controlled by an individual player count as being controlled by their coalition.

FIGHTING THE BATTLE

Instead of each player taking a turn during a Pitched Battle Coalition of Death game, each coalition takes a turn. At the start of the first battle round, the warlord of the coalition that finished setting up all their armies first chooses which coalition has the first turn. At the start of each battle round after the first, the warlords must roll off, and the winner decides which coalition takes the first turn. If the roll-off is a tie, the warlord of the coalition that went first in the last battle round can choose which coalition goes first in the current battle round.

Where individual players would normally alternate taking actions, the coalitions alternate taking actions, with each player in the coalition being allowed to carry them out. For example, in the combat phase, each player in one coalition can attack with 1 of their units, then each player in the other coalition, and so on.

The same principle applies during set-up. For example, if you are fighting a battle where the players

take turns to set up units, then in a Pitched Battle Coalition of Death game, the coalitions take turns to set up, with each player in that coalition setting up 1 unit when it is their coalition's turn to do so. In addition, once all units in one coalition have been set up, the coalitions stop alternating setting up units and the other coalition sets up the rest of its units.

Lastly, rules that refer to the 'opposing player' or 'opponent' are treated as referring to the 'opposing coalition' instead. For example, when a **WIZARD** casts a spell, the opposing coalition can attempt to unbind that spell, following the normal rules for doing so, rather than each player on the opposing coalition making an attempt to unbind that spell.

COALITION MATRIX

The following Coalition Matrix shows the individual armies that can form a coalition in a Pitched Battle Coalition of Death game. The restrictions that your coalition will face on the battlefield will be determined by the hostility of its alliance. Use the key to find out which armies your allegiance can form a coalition with.

Battle-forged coalitions are armies that have formed strong bonds over their numerous tests in combat, while fractious coalitions operate with a degree of caution and always keep an eye on their supposed 'allies'. A desperate coalition is the most strained form of alliance, where trust is as scarce as warriors willing to fight alongside sworn foes.

Legend: ◉ = battle-forged · ✖ = fractious · ◣ = desperate · ▢ = no coalition

	SE	CoS	FS	KO	LRL	DoK	ID	Sylv	Sera	StD	BoK	DoT
Stormcast Eternals	◉	◉	◉	◉	◉	◉	◣	◉	◉	✖	✖	✖
Cities of Sigmar	◉	◉	◉	◉	◣	◣	◣	◣	◣	✖	✖	✖
Fyreslayers	◉	◉	◉	◉	◣	◣	◣	◣	◣	▢	▢	▢
Kharadron Overlords	◉	◉	◉	◉	◣	◣	◣	◣	◣	✖	✖	✖
Lumineth Realm-lords	◉	◣	◣	◣	◉	◉	◣	◉	◣	✖	✖	✖
Daughters of Khaine	◉	◣	◣	◣	◉	◉	◣	◉	◣	✖	✖	✖
Idoneth Deepkin	◣	◣	◣	◣	◣	◣	◉	◣	◣	✖	✖	✖
Sylvaneth	◉	◣	◣	◣	◉	◉	◣	◉	◣	✖	✖	✖
Seraphon	◉	◣	◣	◣	◣	◣	◣	◣	◉	✖	✖	✖
Slaves to Darkness	✖	✖	◣	✖	✖	✖	✖	✖	✖	◉	◉	◉
Blades of Khorne	✖	✖	◣	✖	✖	✖	✖	✖	✖	◉	◉	◉
Disciples of Tzeentch	✖	✖	◣	✖	✖	✖	✖	✖	✖	◉	◉	◉
Maggotkin of Nurgle	✖	✖	◣	✖	✖	✖	✖	✖	✖	◉	◉	◣
Hedonites of Slaanesh	✖	✖	◣	✖	✖	✖	✖	✖	✖	◉	◣	◉
Beasts of Chaos	✖	✖	◣	✖	✖	✖	✖	✖	✖	◉	◉	◉
Skaven	✖	✖	✖	✖	✖	✖	✖	✖	✖	◣	◣	◣
Legions of Nagash	▢	▢	◣	◣	▢	▢	▢	▢	▢	▢	▢	▢
Nighthaunt	▢	▢	◣	◣	▢	▢	▢	▢	▢	▢	▢	▢
Ossiarch Bonereapers	▢	▢	◣	◣	▢	▢	▢	▢	▢	▢	▢	▢
Flesh-eater Courts	▢	▢	▢	▢	▢	▢	▢	▢	◣	◣	◣	◣
Orruk Warclans	▢	▢	▢	▢	▢	▢	▢	▢	▢	▢	▢	▢
Ogor Mawtribes	◣	◣	◣	◣	◣	◣	◣	◣	◣	◣	◣	◣
Gloomspite Gitz	◣	◣	✖	✖	◣	◣	◣	◣	◣	◣	◣	◣
Sons of Behemat	◣	◣	◣	◣	◣	◣	◣	◣	◣	◣	◣	◣

KEY

No coalition possible	Fractious coalition
Battle-forged coalition	Desperate coalition

Legend codes used below: ☠ = No coalition possible · ◉ = Battle-forged coalition · ▰ = Fractious coalition · ▮ = Desperate coalition

	MoN	HoS	BoC	Skav	LoN	NH	OB	FEC	OW	OM	GG	SoB
Stormcast Eternals	☠	☠	☠	☠	▮	▮	▮	▮	▰	▰	▮	▰
Cities of Sigmar	☠	☠	☠	☠	▮	▮	▮	▮	▰	▰	▮	▰
Fyreslayers	▮	▮	▮	☠	▰	▰	▰	▰	▰	▰	☠	▰
Kharadron Overlords	☠	☠	☠	☠	▰	▮	▮	▮	▰	▰	☠	▰
Lumineth Realm-lords	☠	☠	☠	☠	▮	▮	▮	▮	▮	▮	▮	▮
Daughters of Khaine	☠	☠	☠	☠	▮	▮	▮	▮	▮	▮	▮	▮
Idoneth Deepkin	☠	☠	☠	☠	▮	▮	▮	▮	▮	▮	▮	▮
Sylvaneth	☠	☠	☠	☠	▮	▮	▮	▮	▮	▮	▮	▮
Seraphon	☠	☠	☠	☠	▮	▮	▮	▮	▮	▮	▮	▮
Slaves to Darkness	◉	◉	◉	▰	▮	▮	▮	▰	▰	▰	▮	▰
Blades of Khorne	◉	▰	◉	▰	▮	▮	▮	▰	▰	▰	▮	▰
Disciples of Tzeentch	▰	◉	◉	▰	▰	▮	▮	▮	▰	▰	▮	▰
Maggotkin of Nurgle	◉	◉	◉	▰	▮	▮	▮	▮	▰	▰	▮	▰
Hedonites of Slaanesh	◉	◉	◉	▰	▮	▮	▮	▮	▰	▰	▮	▰
Beasts of Chaos	◉	◉	◉	▰	▮	▮	▮	▰	▰	▰	▰	▰
Skaven	▰	▰	▰		▮	▮	▮	▰	▰	▰	▮	▰
Legions of Nagash	▮	▮	▮	▮	◉	◉	◉	◉	▮	▮	▮	▮
Nighthaunt	▮	▮	▮	▮	◉	◉	◉	◉	▮	▮	▮	▮
Ossiarch Bonereapers	▮	▮	▮	▮	◉	◉	◉	◉	▮	▮	▮	▮
Flesh-eater Courts	▰	▰	▰	▰	◉	◉	◉	◉	▰	▰	▰	▰
Orruk Warclans	▮	▮	▮	▮	▮	▮	▮	▮	◉	◉	◉	◉
Ogor Mawtribes	▰	▰	▰	▰	▰	▰	▰	▰	◉	◉	◉	◉
Gloomspite Gitz	▮	▮	▮	▰	▰	▰	▰	▰	◉	◉	◉	◉
Sons of Behemat	▰	▰	▰	▰	▰	▰	▰	▰	◉	◉	◉	◉

REALM OF BATTLE RULES

In matched play games, you will choose which Mortal Realm you and your opponent will be fighting in. This will determine the Realm of Battle rules that will apply to the battle, including realmscape features and realmsphere magic as well as unique command abilities and artefacts of power.

After picking a battleplan to use, you must pick a Mortal Realm for the battle to take place in. The players roll off and the winner picks the Mortal Realm for the battle. On pages 102-107, you will find Realm of Battle rules for each of the Mortal Realms to be used in a matched play game.

If you decide that your army is from a specific Mortal Realm and wish to make one of your artefacts of power a realm artefact, you must pick the realm artefact for your chosen Mortal Realm from the following pages, instead of using an artefact from *Malign Sorcery*.

REALM OF BATTLE: AQSHY, THE REALM OF FIRE

The following Realm of Battle rules are used for matched play battles fought in the Mortal Realm of Aqshy, also known as the Realm of Fire.

REALMSPHERE MAGIC
Fireball: *The wizard claps their hands, conjuring a small orb of flame that they hurl at the foe.*

Fireball has a casting value of 5. If successfully cast, pick 1 enemy unit within 18" of the caster and visible to them. If that enemy unit has 1 model, it suffers 1 mortal wound; if it has 2-9 models, it suffers D3 mortal wounds; and if it has 10 or more models, it suffers D6 mortal wounds.

REALMSCAPE FEATURE
Burning Lands: *The lands of Aqshy are forever brimming with volatile power. As the fires of battle rage,*

this energy magnifies and can even erupt, with lethal effect to anyone unfortunate enough to be nearby.

Terrain features (including faction terrain) have the Volcanic scenery rule (pg 75) in addition to any other scenery rules that they have.

REALM ARTEFACT
Incandescent Rageblade: *In battle, the emberstone crystal set into this sword glows bright, granting the wielder bursts of killing fury.*

Pick 1 of the bearer's melee weapons. If the unmodified hit roll for an attack made by that weapon

is 6, that attack scores 2 hits on the target instead of 1. Make a wound and save roll for each hit.

REALM COMMAND
Blazing Fervour: *In Aqshy, fiery tempers are stoked to lend a warrior formidable endurance.*

You can use this command ability at the start of your hero phase. If you do so, pick 1 friendly unit wholly within 12" of a friendly **Hero**. Add 1 to run and charge rolls made for that unit until your next hero phase. The same unit cannot benefit from this command ability more than once per phase.

REALM OF BATTLE: CHAMON, THE REALM OF METAL

The following Realm of Battle rules are used for matched play battles fought in the Mortal Realm of Chamon, also known as the Realm of Metal.

REALMSPHERE MAGIC

Metamorphic Warding: *Through tapping into the ever-changing magical properties of Chamon, the caster compels the armour and hide of their allies to become as strong as unyielding sigmarite.*

Metamorphic Warding has a casting value of 7. If successfully cast, pick 1 friendly unit wholly within 12" of the caster and visible to them. Add 1 to save rolls for attacks that target that unit until the start of your next hero phase.

REALMSCAPE FEATURE

Transmutative Lands: *Alchemical by nature and further warped by the power of Tzeentch, the lands of Chamon are prone to shift and alter* on a whim, hampering the advance of even the most determined army.

Terrain features (including faction terrain) have the Entangling scenery rule (pg 75) in addition to any other scenery rules that they have.

REALM ARTEFACT

Plate of Perfect Protection: *One of the many mystical artefacts forged by the lost artificers of Metallurgica, the steel of this armour is alloyed with Chamonic quicksilver, allowing it to subtly reform and ward off all but the truest strikes.*

If a weapon used for an attack that targets the bearer has a Rend characteristic of -1, change the Rend characteristic for that attack to '-'.

REALM COMMAND

Living Blades: *In Chamon, each weapon seems to take on a life of its own. When guided by a steely-eyed warrior, they strike at the foe with unerring accuracy.*

You can use this command ability in the combat phase. If you do so, pick 1 friendly unit wholly within 12" of a friendly **Hero**. Until your next hero phase, add 1 to hit rolls for attacks made with melee weapons by that unit if it made a charge move in the same turn.

REALM OF BATTLE: GHUR, THE REALM OF BEASTS

The following Realm of Battle rules are used for matched play battles fought in the Mortal Realm of Ghur, also known as the Realm of Beasts.

REALMSPHERE MAGIC

Wildform: *The wizard transforms their allies into swift-moving bestial forms.*

Wildform has a casting value of 5. If successfully cast, pick 1 friendly unit within 12" of the caster and visible to them. Add 2 to run and charge rolls made for that unit until the start of your next hero phase.

REALMSCAPE FEATURE

Savage Lands: *The lands of Ghur are primal and perilous beyond compare; even the rocks and trees will eagerly devour the unwary, if given a chance.*

Terrain features (including faction terrain) have the Deadly scenery rule (pg 75) in addition to any other scenery rules that they have.

REALM ARTEFACT

Predator's Torc: *When this amber-bronze torc is bound tightly around a limb, the wearer becomes filled with the savage energy of the hunt.*

You can re-roll charge rolls for the bearer.

REALM COMMAND

Feral Roar: *When the wild animus of Ghur fills their bestial souls, monsters of all shapes and sizes will fight on without consideration of injury or pain.*

You can use this command ability in your hero phase. If you do so, pick 1 friendly **MONSTER** wholly within 12" of a friendly **HERO**. Until the end of the battle round, when you look up a value on that model's damage table, that **MONSTER** is treated as if it has suffered 0 wounds.

REALM OF BATTLE: GHYRAN, THE REALM OF LIFE

The following Realm of Battle rules are used for matched play battles fought in the Mortal Realm of Ghyran, also known as the Realm of Life.

REALMSPHERE MAGIC

Shield of Thorns: *At the caster's command, crawling brambles burst from the ground, forming a living barrier around their allies and tearing apart any who approach with malicious intent.*

Shield of Thorns has a casting value of 5. If successfully cast, pick 1 friendly unit wholly within 18" of the caster and visible to them. Until your next hero phase, any enemy unit that finishes a charge move within 3" of that unit suffers D3 mortal wounds. The same friendly unit cannot be picked as the target of this spell more than once per turn.

REALMSCAPE FEATURE

Verdant Lands: *Life blooms eternal in Ghyran, its energies blessing the lands with cyclical regrowth.*

Terrain features (including faction terrain) have the Healing scenery rule (pg 75) in addition to any other scenery rules that they have.

REALM ARTEFACT

Everspring Diadem: *The powers of this oaken crown can soon heal even the most crippling of wounds.*

In your hero phase, you can heal 1 wound allocated to the bearer.

REALM COMMAND

Command the Land: *In Ghyran, even the landscape can be bent to your will.*

You can use this command ability at the end of your hero phase. If you do so, 1 friendly **HERO** can attempt to cast Shield of Thorns, even if they are not a **WIZARD** and even if the spell has already been attempted in the same hero phase. If that **HERO** is a **WIZARD**, using this command ability allows them to attempt to cast Shield of Thorns in addition to any other spells they have already attempted to cast and even if Shield of Thorns has been attempted in the same hero phase.

REALM OF BATTLE: HYSH, THE REALM OF LIGHT

The following Realm of Battle rules are used for Matched Play battles fought in the Mortal Realm of Hysh, also known as the Realm of Light.

REALMSPHERE MAGIC

Purity of Defence: *The wizard bathes their allies in a column of brilliant white light, increasing their speed of thought and reaction time.*

Purity of Defence has a casting value of 5. If successfully cast, pick 1 friendly unit wholly within 12" of the caster and visible to them. You can re-roll save rolls of 1 for attacks that target that unit until the start of you next hero phase.

REALMSCAPE FEATURE

Dazzling Lands: *The lands of Hysh still shine with lambent brilliance. Those who stare into the radiant glow for too long may find themselves blinded just when they need their vision most.*

Terrain features (including faction terrain) have the Mystical scenery rule (pg 75) in addition to any other scenery rules that they have.

REALM ARTEFACT

Syari Trueblade: *Crafted by the aelven mage-artisans of Hysh, this crystalline blade seeks out the enemy with peerless accuracy.*

You can re-roll hit rolls of 1 for attacks made with a melee weapon by the bearer.

REALM COMMAND

All-seeing Enlightenment: *The Realm of Light is a place of purity and enlightenment. Should a warrior focus their mind, they will find themselves able to deduce and thwart even the most cunningly laid ambushes.*

You can use this command ability in your hero phase. If you do so, pick 1 friendly unit wholly within 12" of a friendly **Hero**. Do not apply the cover modifier to save rolls for attacks made by that unit until the start of your next hero phase.

REALM OF BATTLE: SHYISH, THE REALM OF DEATH

The following Realm of Battle rules are used for matched play battles fought in the Mortal Realm of Shyish, also known as the Realm of Death.

REALMSPHERE MAGIC

Ripples of the Necroquake: *It was from the dark heart of Shyish that the necroquake erupted across creation. Those skilled in the arcane arts can tap into this power to call forth lingering magical manifestations with greater ease.*

Ripples of the Necroquake has a casting value of 7. If successfully cast, until the end of that phase, add 1 to casting rolls made for friendly **WIZARDS** if the casting roll is for an endless spell.

REALMSCAPE FEATURE

Terminal Lands: *Even the sorceries of the Arcanum Optimar cannot escape the grasp of Shyish forever.*

Terrain features (including faction terrain) have the Nullification scenery rule (pg 75) in addition to any other scenery rules that they have.

REALM ARTEFACT

Gravesand Brooch: *This morbid item of jewellery is filled with fine particles of gravesand. One who wears it overlong slowly becomes more akin to the dead than the living and is equally hard to slay.*

You can re-roll save rolls of 1 for attacks that target the bearer.

REALM COMMAND

Amethyst Aura: *Those who fight in the Realm of Death have one foot already in the afterlife and can shrug off the most grievous injuries.*

You can use this command ability in your hero phase. If you do so, pick 1 friendly unit wholly within 12" of a friendly **HERO**. Until the end of that battle round, roll a dice each time you allocate a wound or mortal wound to that unit. On a 6, that wound or mortal wound is negated.

REALM OF BATTLE: ULGU, THE REALM OF SHADOW

The following Realm of Battle rules are used for matched play battles fought in the Mortal Realm of Ulgu, also known as the Realm of Shadow.

REALMSPHERE MAGIC

Judgement of Shadow: *The shadows of Ulgu are alive, and they hunger. By speaking thirteen whispered words of power, one for each of the realm's great Dominions, a caster can bid the darkness to swallow up their enemies.*

Judgement of Shadow has a casting value of 7. If successfully cast, pick 1 enemy unit within 12" of the caster that is visible to them and roll 7 dice. For each roll that is less than that unit's unmodified Save characteristic, that unit suffers 1 mortal wound. If the target has an unmodified Save characteristic of '-', it suffers 1 mortal wound for each 2+ instead.

REALMSCAPE FEATURE

Penumbral Lands: *The all-consuming shadows of Ulgu can obscure even the mightiest foe's advance, as many unwary warriors have discovered to their cost.*

Terrain features (including faction terrain) have the Overgrown scenery rule (pg 75) in addition to any other scenery rules that they have.

REALM ARTEFACT

Trickster's Foil: *This phantasmal weapon is never quite where it appears to be, and as such it is capable of inflicting truly horrific wounds on the unprepared.*

You can re-roll wound rolls of 1 for attacks made with a melee weapon by the bearer.

REALM COMMAND

On Me!: *The champion imposes their will on nearby allies, commanding them to reform amidst the enshrouding darkness of Ulgu.*

You can use this command ability once per battle, at the end of your movement phase. If you do so, pick 1 friendly unit wholly within 18" of a friendly **HERO**. Remove that unit from the battlefield and then set it up again wholly within 6" of that friendly **HERO** and more than 9" from any enemy units.

MATCHED PLAY AUXILIARY OBJECTIVES

Auxiliary Objectives are matched-play-focused secondary goals that are designed to test the strategic acumen of any general in Warhammer Age of Sigmar.

In a matched play game, after set-up is complete but before the players determine who has the first turn, each player must pick 2 Auxiliary Objectives to apply to their army for the battle. Once both players have picked their Auxiliary Objectives, they must reveal them to each other simultaneously.

In a matched play game, if you complete more Auxiliary Objectives than your opponent, you count the result of a **draw** for the battle as a **minor victory** instead.

STARTING ARMIES
Several Auxiliary Objectives refer to a player's **starting army**. A player's starting army is made up of the units from the army that were set up before the first battle round, including any reserve units. Units that are added to a player's army after the battle has begun are not included, and neither are units that have been destroyed and subsequently returned to play.

Note that unless an Auxiliary Objective specifically refers to the player's starting army, any unit that meets the specifications is eligible to complete the auxiliary objective.

UNIT TYPES AND POINTS VALUES
Sometimes an Auxiliary Objective will refer to a type of unit. This information is listed in its Pitched Battle profile.

The Aggressor: You complete this Auxiliary Objective if you control all of the objectives wholly within your opponent's territory (this does not include objectives located on the borderline of a territory).

Assassinate: When you reveal this Auxiliary Objective, your opponent must pick 1 unit in their starting army that is a **Hero**. You complete this Auxiliary Objective if that **Hero** is slain before the end of the battle.

The Bait: When you reveal this Auxiliary Objective, you must pick 1 friendly unit in your starting army. You complete this Auxiliary Objective if that unit is destroyed by an enemy unit before the end of the third battle round.

Cornered: You complete this Auxiliary Objective if you have 2 or more friendly units within 3" of the same enemy **Hero** at the end of any turn.

Defender: You complete this Auxiliary Objective if there are no enemy units wholly within your territory at the end of the battle.

Domination: You complete this Auxiliary Objective if 3 or more enemy units are destroyed in the same turn.

Grudge: When you reveal this Auxiliary Objective, you must pick 1 enemy **Hero** in your opponent's starting army and 1 friendly **Hero** in your starting army. You complete this Auxiliary Objective if that enemy **Hero** is slain by an attack made with a melee weapon by that friendly **Hero**.

Headhunter: You complete this Auxiliary Objective if all of the Leader units in your opponent's starting army are destroyed before the end of the battle.

Invader: You complete this Auxiliary Objective if, at the end of the battle, you have more friendly units wholly within your opponent's territory than your opponent has wholly within your territory.

Marked for Death: When you reveal this Auxiliary Objective, your opponent must pick 1 unit in their starting army that is not a **Hero**. You complete this Auxiliary Objective if that unit is destroyed before the end of the battle.

Mass Panic: You complete this Auxiliary Objective if 2 or more different enemy units fail a battleshock test in the same battle round.

Overwhelm: You complete this Auxiliary Objective if an enemy **Hero** is slain by an attack made with a melee weapon by a friendly Battleline unit.

Pillage: When you reveal this Auxiliary Objective, you must pick 1 terrain feature wholly within your opponent's territory. You complete this Auxiliary Objective if you have a friendly unit with a combined Wounds characteristic of 5 or more within 3" of that terrain feature at the end of any battle round. This Auxiliary Objective cannot be completed using a unit that was set up on the battlefield in the same battle round.

Prey on the Weak: You complete this Auxiliary Objective if all of the Battleline units in your opponent's starting army are destroyed before the end of the battle.

Prized Possession: When you reveal this Auxiliary Objective, you must pick 1 friendly **Hero** with an artefact of power in your starting army. You complete this Auxiliary Objective if that **Hero** has not been slain at the end of the battle.

Seize Ground: When you reveal this Auxiliary Objective, you must pick 1 terrain feature that is not within your territory. You complete this Auxiliary Objective if you have 1 or more friendly units within 3" of that terrain feature at the end of the fourth battle round.

Territorial: When you reveal this Auxiliary Objective, you must pick 1 objective on the battlefield. You complete this Auxiliary Objective if you control that objective at the end of 2 consecutive battle rounds.

Vengeful Counter: You complete this Auxiliary Objective if any enemy units are destroyed in the same turn that any friendly units are destroyed.

CONQUEST
UNBOUND

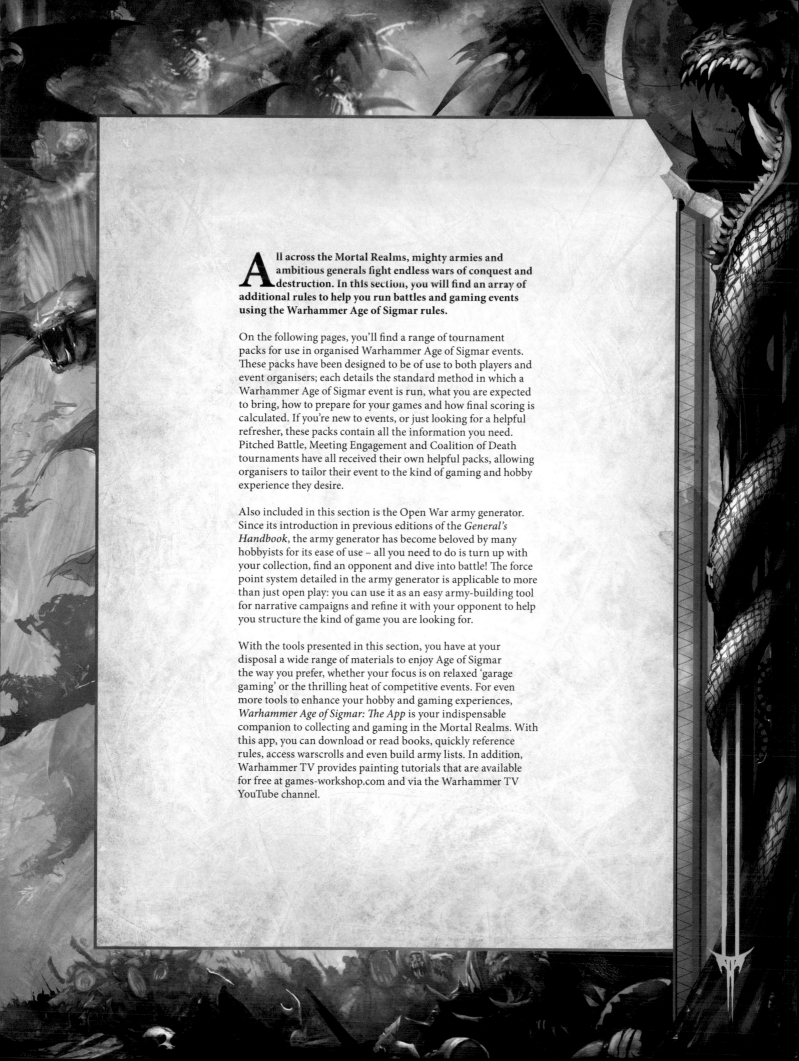

All across the Mortal Realms, mighty armies and ambitious generals fight endless wars of conquest and destruction. In this section, you will find an array of additional rules to help you run battles and gaming events using the Warhammer Age of Sigmar rules.

On the following pages, you'll find a range of tournament packs for use in organised Warhammer Age of Sigmar events. These packs have been designed to be of use to both players and event organisers; each details the standard method in which a Warhammer Age of Sigmar event is run, what you are expected to bring, how to prepare for your games and how final scoring is calculated. If you're new to events, or just looking for a helpful refresher, these packs contain all the information you need. Pitched Battle, Meeting Engagement and Coalition of Death tournaments have all received their own helpful packs, allowing organisers to tailor their event to the kind of gaming and hobby experience they desire.

Also included in this section is the Open War army generator. Since its introduction in previous editions of the *General's Handbook*, the army generator has become beloved by many hobbyists for its ease of use – all you need to do is turn up with your collection, find an opponent and dive into battle! The force point system detailed in the army generator is applicable to more than just open play: you can use it as an easy army-building tool for narrative campaigns and refine it with your opponent to help you structure the kind of game you are looking for.

With the tools presented in this section, you have at your disposal a wide range of materials to enjoy Age of Sigmar the way you prefer, whether your focus is on relaxed 'garage gaming' or the thrilling heat of competitive events. For even more tools to enhance your hobby and gaming experiences, *Warhammer Age of Sigmar: The App* is your indispensable companion to collecting and gaming in the Mortal Realms. With this app, you can download or read books, quickly reference rules, access warscrolls and even build army lists. In addition, Warhammer TV provides painting tutorials that are available for free at games-workshop.com and via the Warhammer TV YouTube channel.

PITCHED BATTLE TOURNAMENT PACK

The following rules are used for the Pitched Battle tournaments that we run ourselves. They can be used as written in your own tournaments or modified as you see fit – as long as all attendees are made aware of any changes.

PITCHED BATTLE TOURNAMENT RULES

The following rules apply to Warhammer Age of Sigmar Pitched Battle tournaments, unless noted otherwise in the tournament rules pack:

1   The tournament will use the core rules – including those pertaining to allegiance abilities and warscroll battalions – and the Pitched Battle rules from the latest *General's Handbook*, including Realm of Battle rules and Auxiliary Objectives. In addition, it will use the rules for endless spells from *Malign Sorcery*.

2   In order to take part in a Pitched Battle tournament, you must bring along a painted army of Citadel Miniatures mounted on the recommended bases. You'll also need dice, a tape measure, all of the rules for the army you are using and copies of your army roster.

3   The army you use must be chosen using the Pitched Battle rules up to a points total of 2,000 points. You can bring along additional painted models to allow you to summon units to the battlefield and to ensure you have suitable models should certain rules or abilities require you to set up an extra unit or replace a model with a different one. You must use the same army and additional models for all of the games you play in the tournament.

4   When you arrive at the event, you must register. You will be given a name badge, a player number and a copy of the Player's Code (pg 5), and you must give a copy of your army roster to the event organisers.

5   Terrain for the battles will be provided and set up by the tournament organisers. All terrain features will be scenery models from the Games Workshop range and will use the rules from their scenery warscroll (scenery warscrolls can be downloaded from the Games Workshop website).

6   You must pick 3 different Auxiliary Objectives (pg 108-109) in each round of the tournament. The Auxiliary Objectives you pick for each round will be recorded on your opponent's results form (see point 10). If you complete 1 or more Auxiliary Objectives, you will receive a bonus to your points score for the game, but you will not count a **draw** as a **minor victory**. You cannot pick the same Auxiliary Objective more than once during the tournament.

7   You will play 3 Pitched Battle games in a short tournament and 5 Pitched Battle games in a long tournament. The time limit for each game is 2 ½ hours.

8   Fifteen minutes before the start of each round, the tournament organisers will tell you which Pitched Battle battleplan is to be used in that round and in which realm the battles in that round are taking place.

9   In the first round, you will play against a randomly selected opponent. In each subsequent round, the players will be ranked according to the number of points they have scored for winning games (when scores are tied, all players with the same score will be ranked in a random order). The first-ranked player will play against the second-ranked player, the third-ranked player will play against the fourth-ranked player, and so on.

10   After each round, you must fill in a results form with both players' names and player numbers, the result your opponent achieved at the end of the battle (note that a player suffers a **minor loss** if their opponent wins a **minor victory** and a **major loss** if their opponent wins a **major victory**), your opponent's Auxiliary Objectives and if they completed them, and the painting and etiquette scores for your opponent. Then add up your opponent's total score.

11   After each round, you will receive points for how well you did in the battle (up to 60 points). To this will be added your painting score for that round (up to 20 points), your etiquette score for that round (up to 5 points), and your score for completing your Auxiliary Objectives in that round (up to 15 points). The maximum possible score for a single round is therefore 100 points. Note that any additional models you bring are included when the painting score for your army is evaluated.

12   The winner of the tournament will be decided by adding together the points each player received in each round. In the

case of a tie, the total number of Auxiliary Objectives completed by the tied players will be used as the first tiebreaker; the total etiquette scores of any remaining tied players will be used as the second tiebreaker; and the total painting scores of any remaining tied players will be used as the third tiebreaker. If any players still remain tied, then the player with the best-painted army in the opinion of the organisers is the winner.

PITCHED BATTLE SHORT SCHEDULE
- 09:00-10:00 – Registration
- 10:00-12:30 – First Round
- 13:30-16:00 – Second Round
- 16:30-19:00 – Third Round
- 19:30 – Results & Awards
- 20:00 – Tournament Ends

PITCHED BATTLE LONG SCHEDULE
Day 1
- 09:00-10:00 – Registration
- 10:00-12:30 – First Round
- 13:30-16:00 – Second Round
- 16:30-19:00 – Third Round

Day 2
- 10:00-12:30 – Fourth Round
- 13:30-16:00 – Fifth Round
- 16:30 – Results & Awards
- 17:00 – Tournament Ends

RESULTS FORM

Round (circle): 1 2 3 4 5

Opponent's Name: _____   **Opponent's Player Number:** _____

Opponent's Result (tick 1 result):
- ☐ Major Victory (60 pts)
- ☐ Minor Victory (40 pts)
- ☐ Draw (30 pts)
- ☐ Minor Loss (20 pts)
- ☐ Major Loss (0 pts)

Auxiliary Objectives Attempted by Opponent (write the names of the Auxiliary Objectives that were attempted and tick the result):

- ☐ Opponent completed 1 Auxiliary Objective (5 pts)
- ☐ Opponent completed 2 Auxiliary Objectives (10 pts)
- ☐ Opponent completed 3 Auxiliary Objectives (15 pts)
- ☐ Opponent did not complete any Auxiliary Objectives (0 pts)

OPPONENT'S SIGNATURE: _____

Opponent's Painting (tick all that apply to your opponent's army):
- ☐ All models were fully painted to a Battle Ready standard (15 pts)
- ☐ All bases were fully painted to a Battle Ready standard, and all base rims were painted a consistent colour (5 pts)

Opponent's Etiquette (tick all that apply to your opponent):
- ☐ Opponent arrived before the round started (1 pt)
- ☐ Opponent introduced themselves in a friendly manner and made a respectful gesture, such as offering a handshake or fist bump, after the game (2 pts)
- ☐ Opponent showed you a copy of their roster (1 pt)
- ☐ Opponent had all of the Citadel Miniatures, dice, measuring instruments and rules that they needed in order to play the game (1 pt)

OPPONENT'S TOTAL SCORE: _____

Your Name: _____   **Your Player Number:** _____

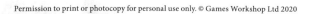

MEETING ENGAGEMENT TOURNAMENT PACK

The following rules are used for the Meeting Engagement tournaments that we run ourselves. They can be used as written in your own tournaments or modified as you see fit – as long as all attendees are made aware of any changes.

MEETING ENGAGEMENT TOURNAMENT RULES

The following rules apply to Warhammer Age of Sigmar Meeting Engagement tournaments, unless noted otherwise in the tournament rules pack:

1   The tournament will use the core rules – including those pertaining to allegiance abilities and warscroll battalions – and the Meeting Engagement rules from the latest *General's Handbook*, including Realm of Battle rules and Auxiliary Objectives. In addition, it will use the rules for endless spells from *Malign Sorcery*.

2   In order to take part in a Meeting Engagement tournament, you must bring along a painted army of Citadel Miniatures mounted on the recommended bases. You'll also need dice, a tape measure, all of the rules for the army you are using and copies of your army roster.

3   The army you use must be chosen using the Meeting Engagement rules up to a points value of 1,000 points. You must also bring 2 painted terrain features (one from the primary list and one from the secondary list, as described in the Meeting Engagement rules). You can bring along additional painted models to allow you to summon units to the battlefield and to ensure you have suitable models should certain rules or abilities require you to set up an extra unit or replace a model with a different one. You must use the same army, terrain features and additional

models for all of the games you play in the tournament.

4   When you arrive at the event, you must register. You will be given a name badge, a player number and a copy of the Player's Code (pg 5), and you must give a copy of your army roster to the event organisers.

5   You must pick 3 different Auxiliary Objectives (pg 108-109) in each round of the tournament. The Auxiliary Objectives you pick for each round will be recorded on your opponent's results form (see point 9). If you complete 1 or more Auxiliary Objectives, you will receive a bonus to your points score for the game, but you will not count a **draw** as a **minor victory**. You cannot pick the same Auxiliary Objective more than once during the tournament.

6   You will play 3 Meeting Engagements in a short tournament and 5 Meeting Engagements in a long tournament. The time limit for each game is 1 ½ hours.

7   Fifteen minutes before the start of each round, the tournament organisers will tell you which Meeting Engagement battleplan is to be used in that round and in which realm the battles in that round are taking place.

8   In the first round, you will play against a randomly selected opponent. In each succeeding round, the players will be ranked according to the number of points they have scored for winning games (when scores are tied, all players with the same score

will be ranked in a random order). The first-ranked player will play against the second-ranked player, the third-ranked player will play against the fourth-ranked player, and so on.

9   After each round, you must fill in a results form with both players' names and player numbers, the result your opponent achieved at the end of the game (note that a player suffers a **minor loss** if their opponent wins a **minor victory** and a **major loss** if their opponent wins a **major victory**), your opponent's Auxiliary Objectives and if they completed them, and the painting and etiquette scores for your opponent. Then add up your opponent's total score.

10   After each round, you will receive points for how well you did in the battle (up to 60 points). To this will be added your painting score for that round (up to 20 points), your etiquette score for that round (up to 5 points), and your score for completing your Auxiliary Objectives in that round (up to 15 points). The maximum possible score for a single round is therefore 100 points. Note that any additional models you bring are included when the painting score for your army is evaluated.

11   The winner of the tournament will be decided by adding together the points each player received in each round. In the case of a tie, the total number of Auxiliary Objectives completed by the tied players will be used as the first tiebreaker; the total etiquette

scores of any remaining tied players will be used as the second tiebreaker; and the total painting scores of any remaining tied players will be used as the third tiebreaker. If any players still remain tied, then the player with the best-painted army in the opinion of the organisers is the winner.

MEETING ENGAGEMENT SHORT SCHEDULE
- 09:00-10:00 – Registration
- 10:00-11:30 – First Round
- 12:00-13:30 – Second Round
- 14:30-16:00 – Third Round
- 16:30 – Results & Awards
- 17:00 – Tournament Ends

MEETING ENGAGEMENT LONG SCHEDULE
- 08:00-09:00 – Registration
- 09:00-10:30 – First Round
- 11:00-12:30 Second Round
- 13:30-15:00 – Third Round
- 15:30-17:00 – Fourth Round
- 17:30-19:00 – Fifth Round
- 19:30 – Results & Awards
- 20:00 – Tournament Ends

RESULTS FORM

Round (circle): 1 2 3 4 5

Opponent's Name: _____ Opponent's Player Number: _____

Opponent's Result (tick 1 result):
- ☐ Major Victory (60 pts)
- ☐ Minor Victory (40 pts)
- ☐ Draw (30 pts)
- ☐ Minor Loss (20 pts)
- ☐ Major Loss (0 pts)

Auxiliary Objectives Attempted by Opponent (write the names of the Auxiliary Objectives that were attempted and tick the result):

- ☐ Opponent completed 1 Auxiliary Objective (5 pts)
- ☐ Opponent completed 2 Auxiliary Objectives (10 pts)
- ☐ Opponent completed 3 Auxiliary Objectives (15 pts)
- ☐ Opponent did not complete any Auxiliary Objectives (0 pts)

OPPONENT'S SIGNATURE:

Opponent's Painting (tick all that apply to your opponent's army):
- ☐ All models were fully painted to a Battle Ready standard (15 pts)
- ☐ All bases were fully painted to a Battle Ready standard, and all base rims were painted a consistent colour (5 pts)

Opponent's Etiquette (tick all that apply to your opponent):
- ☐ Opponent arrived before the round started (1 pt)
- ☐ Opponent introduced themselves in a friendly manner and made a respectful gesture, such as offering a handshake or fist bump, after the game (2 pts)
- ☐ Opponent showed you a copy of their roster (1 pt)
- ☐ Opponent had all of the Citadel Miniatures, dice, measuring instruments and rules that they needed in order to play the game (1 pt)

OPPONENT'S TOTAL SCORE: _____

Your Name: _____ Your Player Number: _____

PITCHED BATTLE COALITION OF DEATH TOURNAMENT PACK

The following section includes new rules for Pitched Battle Coalition of Death tournaments that can be used as written in your own tournaments or modified as you see fit – as long as all attendees are made aware of any changes.

COALITION OF DEATH TOURNAMENT RULES

The following rules apply to Warhammer Age of Sigmar Pitched Battle Coalition of Death tournaments, unless noted otherwise in the tournament rules pack:

1   The tournament will use the core rules – including those pertaining to allegiance abilities and warscroll battalions – and the Pitched Battle Coalition of Death rules from the latest *General's Handbook*, including Realm of Battle rules and Auxiliary Objectives. In addition, it will use the rules for endless spells from *Malign Sorcery*.

2   In order to take part in a Pitched Battle Coalition of Death tournament, you and your teammate must each bring along a painted army of Citadel Miniatures mounted on the recommended bases. You'll also need dice, a tape measure, all of the rules for the army you are using and copies of your army roster.

3   The army you use must be chosen using the Pitched Battle Coalition of Death rules up to a points total of 1,000 points. You can bring along additional painted models to allow you to summon units to the battlefield and to ensure you have suitable models should certain rules or abilities require you to set up an extra unit or replace a model with a different one. You must use the same army and additional models for all of the games you play in the tournament.

4   When you arrive at the event, you must register your coalition. You will each be given a name badge, a player number and a copy of the Player's Code (pg 5), and you must both give a copy of your individual army roster to the event organisers.

5   Terrain for the battles will be provided and set up by the tournament organisers. All terrain features will be scenery models from the Games Workshop range and will use the rules from their scenery warscroll (scenery warscrolls can be downloaded from the Games Workshop website).

6   Your coalition must pick 3 different Auxiliary Objectives (pg 108-109) in each round of the tournament. The Auxiliary Objectives you pick for each round will be recorded on the opposing coalition's results form (see point 10). If your coalition completes 1 or more Auxiliary Objectives, you will receive a bonus to your points score for the game, but you will not count a **draw** as a **minor victory**. Your coalition cannot pick the same Auxiliary Objective more than once during the tournament.

7   You will play 3 Pitched Battle Coalition of Death games in a short tournament, and 5 Pitched Battle Coalition of Death games in a long tournament. The time limit for each game is 2 ½ hours.

8   Fifteen minutes before the start of each round, the tournament organisers will tell you which battleplan is to be used in that round and in which realm the battles in that round are taking place.

9   In the first round, your coalition will play against a randomly selected opponent. In each succeeding round, the coalitions will be ranked according to the number of points they have scored for winning games (when scores are tied, all coalitions with the same score will be ranked in a random order). The first-ranked coalition will play against the second-ranked, the third-ranked will play against the fourth-ranked, and so on.

10   After each round, you must fill in a results form with both coalitions' names and coalition numbers, the result the opposing coalition achieved at the end of the game (note that a coalition suffers a **minor loss** if the opposing coalition wins a **minor victory** and a **major loss** if the opposing coalition wins a **major victory**), the opposing coalition's Auxiliary Objectives and if they completed them, and the painting and etiquette scores for the opposing coalition. Then add up the opposing coalition's total score.

11   After each round, your coalition will receive points for how well you did in the battle (up to 60 points). To this will be added your painting score for that round (up to 20 points), your etiquette score for that round (up to 5 points), and your score for completing your Auxiliary Objectives in that round (up to 15 points). The maximum possible score for a single round is therefore 100 points. Note that any additional models you bring are included when the painting score for your coalition is evaluated.

12 The winner of the tournament will be decided by adding together the points each coalition received in each round. In the case of a tie, the total number of Auxiliary Objectives completed by the tied coalitions will be used as the first tiebreaker; the total etiquette scores of any remaining tied coalitions will be used as the second tiebreaker; and the total painting scores of any remaining tied coalitions will be used as the third tiebreaker. If any coalitions still remain tied, then the coalition with the best-painted armies in the opinion of the organisers is the winner.

PITCHED BATTLE COALITION OF DEATH SHORT SCHEDULE
- 09:00-10:00 – Registration
- 10:00-12:30 – First Round
- 13:30-16:00 – Second Round
- 16:30-19:00 – Third Round
- 19:30 – Results & Awards
- 20:00 – Tournament Ends

PITCHED BATTLE COALITION OF DEATH LONG SCHEDULE
Day 1
- 09:00-10:00 – Registration
- 10:00-12:30 – First Round
- 13:30-16:00 – Second Round
- 16:30-19:00 – Third Round

Day 2
- 10:00-12:30 – Fourth Round
- 13:30-16:00 – Fifth Round
- 16:30 – Results & Awards
- 17:00 – Tournament Ends

RESULTS FORM

Round (circle): 1 2 3 4 5

Opposing Coalition's Name: _____ **Opposing Coalition Number:** _____

Opposing Coalition's Result (tick 1 result):
- ❑ Major Victory (60 pts)
- ❑ Minor Victory (40 pts)
- ❑ Draw (30 pts)
- ❑ Minor Loss (20 pts)
- ❑ Major Loss (0 pts)

Auxiliary Objectives Attempted by Opposing Coalition (write the names of the Auxiliary Objectives that were attempted and tick the result):

- ❑ Opposing coalition completed 1 Auxiliary Objective (5 pts)
- ❑ Opposing coalition completed 2 Auxiliary Objectives (10 pts)
- ❑ Opposing coalition completed 3 Auxiliary Objectives (15 pts)
- ❑ Opposing coalition did not complete any Auxiliary Objectives (0 pts)

OPPOSING COALITION'S SIGNATURES:

Opposing Coalition's Painting (tick all that apply to the opposing coalition's armies):
- ❑ All models were fully painted to a Battle Ready standard (15 pts)
- ❑ All bases were fully painted to a Battle Ready standard, and all base rims were painted a consistent colour (5 pts)

Opposing Coalition's Etiquette (tick all that apply to the opposing coalition):
- ❑ Opposing coalition arrived before the round started (1 pt)
- ❑ Opposing coalition introduced themselves in a friendly manner and made a respectful gesture, such as offering handshakes or fist bumps, after the game (2 pts)
- ❑ Opposing coalition showed you copies of their rosters (1 pt)
- ❑ Opposing coalition had all of the Citadel Miniatures, dice, measuring instruments and rules that they needed in order to play the game (1 pt)

OPPOSING COALITION'S TOTAL SCORE: _____

Your Coalition's Name: _____ **Your Coalition Number:** _____

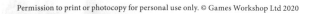

TEAM FORMAT BATTLES

This edition of the *General's Handbook* provides rules that allow you to play Warhammer Age of Sigmar with four-player teams, either as a one-off game or as part of a tournament. The following pages show you how to create a team, the unique roles within each team and how to pair players from opposing teams against one another.

THE ARMIES

To play a Team Format game of Warhammer Age of Sigmar, you will need 8 players divided into 2 teams of 4. Each player must follow the Battlehost Pitched Battle chart restrictions on page 72 when picking their army.

Points, warscroll battalions and Battleline units in each individual army cannot be shared by other armies in your team.

In addition, the following restrictions apply to Team Format armies:

- Each army in a team must have a different allegiance.

- A team cannot include the same warscroll or artefact of power in more than one player's army.

- Any units that are added to a player's army during a game (such as summoned units) are exempt from the above restriction.

Once each army in your team has been selected, you must record each one on an army roster that includes the player's name and team name. All information must be clearly readable for your opponents to understand.

Your roster must include a list of the units, warscroll battalions and endless spells included in your army; what size the units are; the army's allegiance, which units are allies; if you have purchased an extra command point; and which model is the army's general.

Use the notes column for each unit to record the command models you have chosen for it, the spells that are known by the **WIZARDS** in your army, any artefacts or other items wielded by **HEROES** in your army, and which command trait you have chosen for your general.

If your army includes any units that are given keywords when they are set up, such as units with a Mark of Chaos, these must be written down when the unit is added to the roster.

The opposing team will have the opportunity to look over your team's rosters when pairings are determined before the game.

TEAM CAPTAINS

Before any Team Format games are played, each team must nominate 1 player to be the **team captain**.

The team captain has various duties during a Team Format game, including pairing players, collecting and recording team results and taking overall responsibility for their team.

A team captain can also:

- Ask a teammate for updates on an active battle.

- Tell their teammates the results of other battles.

- Handle rules enquiries from teammates.

PAIRINGS

One of the unique qualities of Team Format games is how players from opposing teams are paired against one another. The decisions made here can heavily impact the outcome of your team's performance.

When pairing players, it is important to consider favourable match-ups, i.e. identifying your strongest players and pitting them against suitable opponents in the other team.

In order to pair players for the game, write each player's name and army on individual notecards or pieces of non-transparent paper.

Before the game, the teams have 30 minutes to look over each team's rosters and establish which players will play each other by using the following pairing system:

1. **The Spearhead phase:**
   During this phase, both teams pick 1 army from their team and place the corresponding notecard face down on the table. This is the **spearhead**. Once both teams have done this, flip over and reveal both notecards simultaneously.

2. **The Counter phase:**
   Each team picks 2 other armies from their team in response to the opposing team's spearhead, placing the corresponding notecards face down on the table. These are the **counter**. Once both teams have done this, flip over and reveal all notecards simultaneously.

   After the counters have been revealed, each team picks 1 army from the opposing team's counter to play against their spearhead.

3. The army in each counter that was not picked is paired against the army that was not put forward by the opposing team.

PAIRINGS FOR 6- OR 8-PLAYER TEAMS

The following pairing systems can be used for larger Team Format games.

For a 6-player team game:

1. **The Spearhead phase:**
   During this phase, both teams pick 1 army from their team and place the corresponding notecard face down on the table. This is the **spearhead**. Once both teams have done this, flip over and reveal both notecards simultaneously.

2. **The Counter phase:**
   Each team picks 2 other armies from their team in response to

the opposing team's spearhead, placing the corresponding notecards face down on the table. These are the **counter**. Once both teams have done this, flip over and reveal all notecards simultaneously.

After the counters have been revealed, each team picks 1 army from the opposing team's counter to play against their spearhead.

3. **The Return phase:**
The armies in each counter that were not picked are returned to their respective teams.

4. Repeat the Spearhead and Counter phases (steps 1 and 2) with the remaining armies.

5. The army in each counter that was not picked is paired against the army that was not put forward by the opposing team.

For an 8-player team game, follow the instructions for 6 players, but repeat the Spearhead, Counter and Return phases (steps 1, 2 and 3) before moving on to steps 4 and 5.

BATTLEPLANS
Use the Pitched Battle battleplans on pages 76-87 for a Pitched Battle Team Format game.

AUXILIARY OBJECTIVES
In this format, Auxiliary Objectives (pg 108-109) have the following restrictions per battle:

• Each player must pick 2 Auxiliary Objectives to complete.

• The same Auxiliary Objective cannot be picked more than once across all players in your team.

SCORING
The following scoring system is used in Team Format games to calculate a team's overall score for each battle.

A maximum of 20 points is available to each player for each battle they play. At the end of each battle, each player must record their results with their team captain.

To determine the winner of each battle, use the victory conditions as described in the battleplan, then look up the result in the Points table.

At the end of the game, the points earned by players across all battles will be totalled for each team, and the team that has the most points is the winner.

POINTS TABLE	
Result	**Points**
Major victory	16
Minor victory	12
Draw	8
Minor loss	4
Major loss	0
You completed your Auxiliary Objectives	1 for each completed
Your opponent did not complete their Auxiliary Objectives	1 for each not completed

TIEBREAKERS
In a Team Format game, in addition to having a score value in each battle, Auxiliary Objectives are used as tiebreakers to determine the winning team in a tied game.

If the overall outcome of all battles for both teams results in a **draw**, add up the total number of Auxiliary Objectives completed by each team.

If one team has completed more Auxiliary Objectives, they are declared the winner. If both teams have completed the same number of Auxiliary Objectives, the game is a **draw**.

TEAM FORMAT TOURNAMENT PACK

The following section includes new rules for Team Format tournaments that can be used as written in your own tournaments or modified as you see fit – as long as all attendees are made aware of any changes.

TEAM FORMAT TOURNAMENT RULES

The following rules apply to Warhammer Age of Sigmar Team Format tournaments, unless noted otherwise in the tournament rules pack:

1   The tournament will use the core rules – including those pertaining to allegiance abilities and warscroll battalions – and the Team Format rules from the latest *General's Handbook*, including Realm of Battle rules and Auxiliary Objectives. In addition, it will use the rules for endless spells from *Malign Sorcery*.

2   In order to take part in a Team Format tournament, you and your teammates must each bring along a painted army of Citadel Miniatures mounted on the recommended bases. You'll also need dice, a tape measure, all of the rules for the army you are using and copies of your army roster.

3   The army you use must be chosen using the Team Format rules to a points total of 2,000 points. You can bring along additional painted models to allow you to summon units to the battlefield and to ensure you have suitable models should certain rules or abilities require you to set up an extra unit or replace a model with a different one. You must use the same army and additional models for all of the games you play in the tournament.

4   When you arrive at the event, your team captain must register your team. You will each be given a name badge, a player number and a copy of the Player's Code (pg 5), and you must all give a copy of your army rosters to the event organisers.

5   Terrain for the battles will be provided and set up by the tournament organisers. All terrain features will be scenery models from the Games Workshop range and will use the rules from their scenery warscroll (scenery warscrolls can be downloaded from the Games Workshop website).

6   Each individual player in your team must pick 2 different Auxiliary Objectives (pg 108-109) in each round of the tournament. The Auxiliary Objectives you pick for each round will be recorded on your opponent's results form (see point 10). If an individual player completes 1 or more Auxiliary Objectives, your team will receive a bonus to its points score for the round, but you will not count a **draw** as a **minor victory**. An individual player in a team cannot pick the same Auxiliary Objective more than once during the tournament.

7   Your team will play 3 Team Format battles in a short tournament and 5 Team Format battles in a long tournament. The time limit for each battle is 2 ½ hours.

8   Fifteen minutes before the start of each round, the tournament organisers will tell you which battleplan is to be used in that round and in which realm the battles in that round are taking place.

9   In the first round, your team will play against a randomly selected opponent. In each succeeding round, the teams will be ranked according to the number of points they have scored for winning games (when scores are tied, all teams with the same score will be ranked in a random

order). The first-ranked team will play against the second-ranked team, the third-ranked team will play against the fourth-ranked team, and so on. Teams will have 15 minutes to pair players for the upcoming round (pg 118-119).

10   After each round, each individual player must fill in a results form with both players' names and team numbers, the result their opponent achieved at the end of the game (note that a player suffers a **minor loss** if their opponent wins a **minor victory**, and a **major loss** if their opponent wins a **major victory**), their opponent's Auxiliary Objectives and if they completed them, and the painting and etiquette scores for their opponent. Then they add up their opponent's total score.

11   After each round, each individual player in your team will receive points for how well they did in the battle (up to 16 points). To this will be added their painting score for that round (up to 20 points), their etiquette score for that round (up to 5 points) and their score for completing Auxiliary Objectives in that round (up to 4 points). The maximum possible score for a single round is therefore 45 points. Note that any additional models brought are included when the painting score for the army is evaluated.

12   The winner of the tournament will be decided by adding together the points each team received in each round. In the case of a tie, the total number of Auxiliary Objectives completed by the tied teams will be used as the first tiebreaker; the total etiquette scores of any remaining tied teams will be used as the

second tiebreaker; and the total painting scores of any remaining tied teams will be used as the third tiebreaker. If any teams still remain tied, then the team with the best-painted armies in the opinion of the organisers is the winner.

TEAM FORMAT SHORT SCHEDULE
- 09:00-10:00 – Registration
- 10:00-12:30 – First Round
- 13:30-16:00 – Second Round
- 16:30-19:00 – Third Round
- 19:30 – Results & Awards
- 20:00 – Tournament Ends

TEAM FORMAT LONG SCHEDULE
Day 1
- 09:00-10:00 – Registration
- 10:00-12:30 – First Round
- 13:30-16:00 – Second Round
- 16:30-19:00 – Third Round

Day 2
- 10:00-12:30 – Fourth Round
- 13:30-16:00 – Fifth Round
- 16:30 – Results & Awards
- 17:00 – Tournament Ends

RESULTS FORM

Round (circle):   1   2   3   4   5

Opponent's Name: _____   **Opponent's Player Number:** _____

Opponent's Result (tick 1 result):

☐ Major Victory (16 pts)   ☐ Minor Loss (4 pts)

☐ Minor Victory (12 pts)   ☐ Major Loss (0 pts)

☐ Draw (8 pts)

Auxiliary Objectives Attempted by Opponent (write the names of the Auxiliary Objectives that were attempted):

Number of Auxiliary Objectives your opponent completed: _____ pts

Number of Auxiliary Objectives you did not complete: _____ pts

OPPONENT'S SIGNATURE:

Opponent's Painting (tick all that apply to your opponent's army):

☐ All models were fully painted to a Battle Ready standard (15 pts)   ☐ All bases were fully painted to a Battle Ready standard, and all base rims were painted a consistent colour (5 pts)

Opponent's Etiquette (tick all that apply to your opponent):

☐ Opponent arrived before the round started (1 pt)   ☐ Opponent showed you a copy of their roster (1 pt)

☐ Opponent introduced themselves in a friendly manner and made a respectful gesture, such as offering a handshake or fist bump, after the game (2 pts)   ☐ Opponent had all of the Citadel Miniatures, dice, measuring instruments and rules that they needed in order to play the game (1 pt)

OPPONENT'S TOTAL SCORE: _____

Your Name: _____   Your Player Number: _____

OPEN WAR ARMY GENERATOR

The Open War army generator is designed for players that like the ease and simplicity of open play games and are looking for as much variety in their armies as possible. If you use it, your army need never be exactly the same from one battle to the next.

This generator is intended to be used alongside the Open War battleplan generator tables from the *Warhammer Age of Sigmar Core Book* or the Open War card deck. If both players have agreed to use the battleplan generator, they can agree to use the army generator as well. In addition, both players can agree to use the army generator on its own to generate armies for any kind of open play games. You may also find them useful for generating armies in narrative or matched play games, although they are not designed specifically for that purpose.

The Open War army generator replaces the normal method for picking an army. Instead of having a completely free choice as to which units are used, the generator will help each player pick a balanced force from the units in their collection. This means that, just like a real general, you will not have complete control over the forces under your command. Instead, you will need to know how to get the best from all of the different units in your collection and learn how to meld different combinations of combatants into a potent fighting force.

The Open War army generator makes the process of picking an army quick and simple. All you need to do is bring along a selection of the units from your collection to your game, and the army generator will tell you which ones to use. Alternatively, you can use the generator to pick an army before the game, and then just bring along the units you need when it's time to play.

AGREE FORCE SIZE

To use the army generator, the players must first agree a force size for the battle. The force size can either be small, medium or large. A game with a small force size can be completed in an hour or two, a game with a medium force size will take two or three hours to play, and a game with a large force size will take a full afternoon or evening. We recommend using a small force size for your first game using the generator. The force size you choose will determine the force point limit for each player. Force points can be spent to build your army. The table below shows the force point limit each player has for each force size, and the typical number of units the army will have.

TAILORED FORCE LIMITS (OPTIONAL)

Instead of picking a small, medium or large battle, you can simply choose the force point limit for your game, using the force size table as a guideline.

FORCE SIZE TABLE		
Force Size	**Force Point Limit**	**Typical Number of Units**
Small	15	5-10
Medium	20	8-15
Large	30	10-20

BATTLEPLAN GENERATORS

If you are using the army generator in conjunction with the Open War battleplan generator tables or the Open War cards, the following modifications to the rules for generating a battleplan apply:

- Instead of setting up terrain as described in the core rules, you can use the terrain generator tables in this book (pg 126-127).

- Do not roll on the Ruse or Sudden Death tables in the Core Book until after the armies have been set up, and use the rules below instead of those described in the Open War battleplan generator or the Open War cards.

- Follow the instructions below for setting up your army, instead of those described in the Open War battleplan generator or the Open War cards.

USING THE ARMY GENERATOR

The army generator can either be used as a table that you roll on, or it can be photocopied and cut out into 36 cards that you can then shuffle and draw. If you are rolling on it as a table, roll two dice one after the other, counting the first roll as tens and the second roll as digits. For example, if the first roll was a 3 and the second roll a 4, the army generator roll would be 34. Find the entry on the generator that corresponds to this number. If you are using cards, instead of making a roll, simply draw a card from the shuffled deck.

Each entry on the generator provides a list of one or more units that the player can set up on the battlefield. It will list how many and what type of units you can set up (see Unit Types, opposite) and how many force points those units cost. You do not have to set up all of the units listed, but note that the force points cost is fixed: it does not change if you can't set up all of the units listed or choose not to set up all of the units listed. Any you do not set up are ignored (they do not count as being destroyed).

The players alternate using the army generator, starting with the player who won the roll-off to pick territories. After generating their first list of units, the player picks the units from their collection that correspond to that list and sets them up wholly within their own territory. Then their opponent generates their first list of units, picks the units from their collection that correspond to that list of units and sets them up wholly within their own territory. The players take it in turns to generate, pick and set up units in this manner until both armies have been set up (see Completing Set-up, below).

PRE-BATTLE ARMY GENERATION (OPTIONAL)

If the players wish, they can generate their armies before the battle and just bring along the models they will be using to the game. To do this, the players must write down their rolls, or the cards they draw, and the units that they decide to use, and then they alternate setting up the units in the order they were generated.

UNIT TYPES

Rather than listing specific units, the army generator will tell you what type of unit you can set up. The table below describes each unit type. Remember that all of the models in a unit must be chosen from the same warscroll.

UNIT TYPE TABLE	
Type	**Description**
Horde	A unit of up to 20 models, each with a Wounds characteristic of 1 and a Save characteristic of 6+ or '-'.
Regular	A unit of up to 10 models, each with a Wounds characteristic of 1 and a Save characteristic of 3+, 4+ or 5+.
Elite	A unit of up to 5 models, each with a Wounds characteristic of 2 or 3.
Guard	A unit of up to 3 models, each with a Wounds characteristic of 4 or 5.
Linebreaker	A unit of 1 model with a Wounds characteristic of 6-9 that is not a **Hero**.
Gargantuan	A unit of 1 model that has a Wounds characteristic of 10 or more that is not a **Hero**.
Champion	A **Hero** that is not a **Monster**.
Conqueror	Any **Hero**.

ENDLESS SPELLS

If an endless spell is generated by the army generator, you can pick 1 endless spell of your choice. All **Wizards** in your army know that endless spell, and you can use (and re-use) 1 model of the appropriate type during the battle. If you generate more than 1 endless spell, you must pick a different endless spell each time.

STRENGTHENED UNITS

Some of the units listed will be marked with a '*' symbol. These units can be strengthened with extra models. A strengthened unit can have up to double the number of models listed in its description at a cost of 1 extra force point.

Alternatively, a strengthened unit can have up to triple the number of models listed in its description at a cost of 2 extra force points. For example, if the army generator lists '1 Regular* unit', it can have up to 20 eligible models for 1 extra force point or up to 30 eligible models for 2 extra force points.

SUBSTITUTIONS

If you cannot or do not want to set up one or more of the units listed, you can choose to take a substitute unit instead. Note that you must decide to do this before you set up any units from that list – you can't set up some units and then take a substitute and set up some more.

When you take a substitute, you can pick 1 unit from the list below. Substitute units cost 2 force points each, plus an extra 1 or 2 force points if they are strengthened (see Strengthened Units, above).

Substitutions
1 Horde* unit
1 Regular* unit
1 Elite* unit
1 Guard* unit
1 Linebreaker* unit
1 Champion

COMPLETING SET-UP

During set-up, each player must keep track of the total number of force points they have spent. Once a roll or card results in a player's force points total equalling or exceeding the force point limit for the game, they can set up the units generated by that roll or card, and then their army set-up is complete (they cannot make any further rolls or draw any further cards).

The opposing player can keep on generating and setting up units until a roll or card means that their force points total also equals or exceeds the force point limit for the game, at which point they can set up the units generated by that roll or card and then their army set-up is also complete. A player must also finish setting up if they no longer have any units to set up.

RUSES AND SUDDEN DEATH

After set-up for both armies is complete, compare the players' force points totals. If one player has spent fewer force points than their opponent, that player can roll on the Ruse table in the Core Book. If one army has a force points total that is at least double the other, then the player with the lower total can roll on the Sudden Death table as well as the Ruse table.

ARMY GENERATOR

11
- 1 **Horde*** unit

1 FORCE POINT
*Can be strengthened

12
- 1 **Regular*** unit

1 FORCE POINT
*Can be strengthened

13
- 1 **Elite*** unit

1 FORCE POINT
*Can be strengthened

14
- 1 **Guard*** unit

1 FORCE POINT
*Can be strengthened

15
- 1 **Champion** or 1 **Linebreaker*** unit

1 FORCE POINT
*Can be strengthened

16
- 1 **Endless Spell**

1 FORCE POINT

21
- 1 **Gargantuan** model

2 FORCE POINTS

22
- 2 **Champions**

2 FORCE POINTS

23
- 1 **Champion**
- 1 **Horde*** or **Regular*** unit

2 FORCE POINTS
*Can be strengthened

24
- 1 **Champion**
- 1 **Regular*** or **Elite** unit

2 FORCE POINTS
*Can be strengthened

25
- 1 **Champion**
- 1 **Elite***, **Guard*** or **Linebreaker*** unit

2 FORCE POINTS
*Can be strengthened

26
- 1 **Champion**
- 1 **Endless Spell**

2 FORCE POINTS

31
- 1 **Conqueror**

3 FORCE POINTS

32
- 1 **Champion**
- 1 **Gargantuan** model

3 FORCE POINTS

33
- 1 **Champion**
- 2 **Regular*** or **Horde*** units (in any combination)

3 FORCE POINTS
*Can be strengthened

34
- 1 **Champion**
- 2 **Regular*** or **Elite** units (in any combination)

3 FORCE POINTS
*Can be strengthened

35
- 3 **Horde***, **Regular*** or **Elite** units (in any combination)

3 FORCE POINTS
*Can be strengthened

36
- 1 **Champion**
- 2 **Elite***, **Guard*** or **Linebreaker*** units (in any combination)

3 FORCE POINTS
*Can be strengthened

41
- 1 **Conqueror**
- 1 **Elite***, **Guard*** or **Linebreaker*** unit

4 FORCE POINTS
*Can be strengthened

42
- 1 **Champion**
- 1 **Gargantuan** model

4 FORCE POINTS

43
- 1 **Champion**
- 3 **Horde***, **Regular*** or **Elite** units (in any combination)

4 FORCE POINTS
*Can be strengthened

44
- 3 **Horde*** or **Regular*** units (in any combination)
- 1 **Elite**, **Guard** or **Linebreaker** unit

4 FORCE POINTS
*Can be strengthened

45
- 1 **Champion**
- 2 **Horde*** or **Regular*** units (in any combination)
- 1 **Elite**, **Guard** or **Linebreaker** unit

4 FORCE POINTS
*Can be strengthened

46
- 1 **Conqueror**
- 1 **Elite***, **Guard*** or **Linebreaker*** unit

4 FORCE POINTS
*Can be strengthened

51
- 1 **Conqueror**
- 2 **Elite***, **Guard*** or **Linebreaker*** units (in any combination)

5 FORCE POINTS
*Can be strengthened

52
- 1 **Champion**
- 2 **Gargantuan** models

5 FORCE POINTS

53
- 1 **Champion**
- 3 **Horde*** or **Regular*** units (in any combination)
- 1 **Elite**, **Guard** or **Linebreaker** unit

5 FORCE POINTS
*Can be strengthened

54
- 1 **Champion**
- 3 **Elite*** or **Guard*** units (in any combination)
- 1 **Linebreaker*** unit

5 FORCE POINTS
*Can be strengthened

55
- 1 **Champion**
- 3 **Horde***, **Regular*** or **Elite*** units (in any combination)
- 1 **Guard*** or **Linebreaker*** unit

5 FORCE POINTS
*Can be strengthened

56
- 1 **Conqueror**
- 1 **Horde***, **Regular*** or **Elite*** unit
- 1 **Guard*** or **Linebreaker*** unit

5 FORCE POINTS
*Can be strengthened

61
- 1 **Conqueror**
- 2 **Horde***, **Regular*** or **Elite*** units (in any combination)
- 1 **Guard*** or **Linebreaker*** unit

6 FORCE POINTS
*Can be strengthened

62
- 1 **Conqueror**
- 2 **Champions**
- 1 **Elite*** or **Guard*** unit

6 FORCE POINTS
*Can be strengthened

63
- 1 **Champion**
- 3 **Horde***, **Regular***, **Elite*** or **Guard** units (in any combination)
- 1 **Gargantuan** model or 1 **Linebreaker*** unit

6 FORCE POINTS
*Can be strengthened

64
- 1 **Conqueror**
- 1 **Champion**
- 3 **Elite***, **Guard*** or **Linebreaker*** units (in any combination)

6 FORCE POINTS
*Can be strengthened

65
- 1 **Conqueror**
- 1 **Champion**
- 2 **Horde***, **Regular*** or **Elite*** units (in any combination)
- 1 **Guard*** or **Linebreaker*** unit

6 FORCE POINTS
*Can be strengthened

66
- Up to 6 models/ units of your choice*, as long as no more than 1 is a **Conqueror** and/or a **Gargantuan** model

6 FORCE POINTS
*Eligible units can be strengthened

OPEN WAR TERRAIN

Although you don't need many, or indeed any, terrain features to play Warhammer Age of Sigmar, most players would agree that a battlefield looks better when it is covered with plenty of carefully modelled scenery pieces. On the following pages, you will find various methods for setting up terrain in Open War games.

It is usually best to choose and set up terrain using a method that will create roughly the same advantages and disadvantages for both sides. The following methods are ideal for setting up terrain in Open War games and are designed to be used in conjunction with the Open War battleplan generator in the *Warhammer Age of Sigmar Core Book*, the Open War cards and the Open War army generator on pages 122-125 – although you can use any of these methods in any of your games.

When using these rules, you must set up the terrain before you pick or generate the battleplan you will be using.

The players should agree on the method that appeals the most, or that best suits the game they are going to play, and follow the instructions below. Whatever method you use, the more time and effort you put into creating an attractive battlefield, the more interesting your battles will become.

METHOD 1: PRE-BATTLE TERRAIN SET-UP
One player sets up the terrain on the battlefield. The other player chooses the player's territories for the battle, if there is a choice in the battleplan that is being used. This method is useful when playing at a friend's house, as it allows one player to set up the battlefield before their opponent arrives for the game. As no territories have been decided when the terrain is set up, the player setting up the terrain is not able to favour either side.

METHOD 2: BY HALVES TERRAIN SET-UP
The table is divided in half and each player sets up the terrain in one half of the table. This is suitable for a game at a club where both players arrive at the same time to set up the battlefield. Neither player will know for certain where they will be setting up their units, so neither will have an advantage. This is a good method if you have a limited collection of terrain pieces, as you can divide the terrain roughly equally between each half of the battlefield.

METHOD 3: ALTERNATING TERRAIN SET-UP
The players roll off and then take it in turns to set up terrain features, one at a time, starting with the player who won the roll-off. Terrain features can be set up anywhere on the battlefield. This continues until either all of the available terrain features have been set up, or until one player declares that there is enough terrain on the battlefield and opts not to set up a terrain feature in their turn. The other player can then set up one last terrain feature.

METHOD 4: BY SQUARES TERRAIN SET-UP
Divide the battlefield into 2' by 2' squares. The players roll off and then take it in turns to set up terrain features, one at a time, starting with the player who won the roll-off. In their turn, each player picks a square that does not yet contain a terrain feature or that has not been declared barren (see below) and sets up a terrain feature in that square. Each player can place 2 terrain features in a square once during set up, and each player can place no terrain features in a square once during set up, declaring it **barren**. This continues until either all the available terrain features have been set up, or all squares either contain at least 1 terrain feature or have been declared barren.

TERRAIN GENERATOR TABLE (OPTIONAL)
An alternative to picking the terrain features that are set up is to use the terrain generator table below. Simply roll on the table instead of picking a terrain feature to set up, re-rolling the result if you generate a piece of terrain you don't have.

2D6	Terrain Feature
2-3	Shattered Temple
4	Numinous Occulum
5	Walls and Fences
6	Azyrite Ruins
7	Awakened Wyldwood
8	Ophidian Archway
9	Timeworn Ruins
10	Baleful Realmgate
11	Sigmarite Mausoleum
12	Sigmarite Dais

BESPOKE TERRAIN GENERATOR TABLES
You may prefer to make your own terrain generator table based on the terrain pieces you have in your collection. If you wish to do so, you can download a template from warhammer-community.com.

LANDSCAPE TABLE (OPTIONAL)

Instead of the players having free rein as to where they set up terrain features using methods 1-3, before setting up any terrain, one player can roll on the landscape table, right. The instructions apply to both players. We don't recommend using the landscape table with the 'By Squares' method.

D6   Landscape

1   The first 4 terrain features must be set up within 6" of one of the four corners of the battlefield. Any remaining terrain features can be set up anywhere.

2   Terrain features cannot be set up within 12" of the centre of the battlefield.

3   The first terrain feature must be set up at the centre of the battlefield. Any remaining terrain features must be set up within 8" of a feature that has already been set up.

4-5   The first 4 terrain features must be set up so that one is in each quarter of the battlefield. Any remaining terrain features can be set up anywhere.

6   The first terrain feature must be set up at the centre of the battlefield. Any remaining terrain features must be set up more than 12" from the first.

PITCHED BATTLE ROSTER

Player:		Allegiance:		
Units	Size	Role/Ally	Notes (traits, artefacts, spells, etc.)	Pts
Extra Command Points				
Endless Spell				
Endless Spell				
Warscroll Battalion				
Warscroll Battalion				
TOTAL POINTS				
NOTES				